THE TRUST PROTECTOR

H.K. Finley

ISBN: 978-0-578-68487-1

The Trust Protection is a work of fiction. Names, characters, places, incidents are a product of the author's imagination or used as fiction. Any resemblances to actual persons living or dead, or places, or events is coincidental.

ISBN 978-0-578-68487-1
51000>
9 780578 684871

CHAPTERS

CHAPTER 1 — MITCH STONE

I rode with my two friends three times a week. Hank and Rob rode seven. They didn't have to work eighteen hours a day to get where they were on the financial scoreboard. They were from Little Rock's moldy-money class. I met them through my second wife, Amber, the daughter of a prominent Little Rock physician. If it weren't for her, I wouldn't be friends with them, or a member of Little Rock Country Club.

Hank and Rob were fast, hard riders, and I worked my ass off to keep up with them. I was and wasn't looking forward to the Moab bike adventure and what would be a long tough ride over a three-day weekend. My six mornings a week at the gym with a trainer made my body hard, but it didn't make me quick—that came from riding, and I didn't have the time. I kept up with my buddies by drawing on my determination.

We took a private jet to Moab a day earlier and visited Canyonlands and Arches National Parks, indulged in massages at Sorrel Ranch, where we were staying. The next day, the three of us met up with seven other riders to begin a mountain bike adventure that started at Slick Rock and would end with The Whole Enchilada—a ride that had it all—tough riding and fantastic scenery.

On the third day, I felt a little tired, but looking at the others, I saw I wasn't the only one. I signaled I was going to stop for a piss and would catch up, but in fact I needed a break. I hadn't ridden this hard for this many days in a row since last year and was feeling it in my lower back.

I pulled off and stood for a few minutes to relax my legs. I took a shot of the valley below with my cell to send to Carlotta. She liked that sort of thing, and maybe it would keep her from constantly pinging me. I had my phone in my hand when I began to relieve myself and nearly dropped it when I saw blood instead of urine. My heart raced in my chest and I felt fear creep up my body. I stared at the red splatter hitting the rock and took a photo. Dehydration can cause blood in the urine. I pulled out my water bottle and gulped down the whole thing.

Got on my bike and hoped to catch up to the group by the time they met back at the van. I pushed until I caught up and thought I would vomit. I recognized the effort was my way of chasing away fear.

It was kidney cancer; I just knew it. I would die from it, like Dad had ten years earlier. I wouldn't allow myself to deteriorate in a hospice room—I would kill myself first. I should just go ahead and ride myself off the next cliff. That way it would look like an accident, and my fifteen million dollar insurance policy would still pay. Or maybe crash my helicopter. If I shot myself, those premiums would be wasted. *Shut up, shut up, shut up*, became my mantra as I tried to and finally did manage to control my thoughts.

There was a cooler full of beer in the van and beer is a recovery drink, so I chugged two and another liter of water, hoping when I pissed again it would be clear, but it wasn't. I sent the red stream photo to Elle Hawk, my mother.

"WTF is that" she wrote back.
I texted, "I think I'm fucked like Daddy."

My phone rang. I answered, and Moma said, "I know what you're thinking. Asphalt doesn't smell like money—it smells like cancer. So hold off killing yourself and wait and see if that applies to you." Then she asked if I wanted her to come to Little Rock.

I said, "Not yet." She'd trained to be a nurse eons ago, before walking out of the hospital a few weeks before graduation. Moma knew she didn't have the disposition for nursing, but she'd enjoyed science.

When the diagnosis came a few days later, my voice couldn't hide its fear. I pulled my car over to the side of the road, "Not kidney cancer—bladder." I could hear the ocean moving in the background and knew Moma was at the beach. I looked at my watch. She had probably just finished her morning swim on the North shore of Maui.

Moma said as soon as she saw the picture of my red-tinged urine stream, she knew in her heart her worst fear was coming true. She would be the fourth generation of mothers in her family to lose a son. The family curse had finally come home to roost in her nest. Her sister, Izzy, their mother, their grandmother, and their great-grandmother, all had only sons who died before their mothers. She feared this day for forty-nine years. Her mother lived less than five years after her son died of the flu; her grandmother went to the cemetery every day until she died forty years after her son was killed in an airplane crash; she didn't know about her great grandmother after her son died in a train wreck; her sister, Izzy, seemed okay after her son, Max, died from bladder cancer.

"I know what you're thinking, Moma." And she didn't deny it. All she could think about was her youngest daughter, had an only son, and hoped the curse ended here.

Two weeks later, I came home early from the office the day I got my death sentence and gave my wife the news—her response didn't surprise me. "Well, I told you when you snuck around behind my back and had that vasectomy after I lost our last baby, it would give you cancer. So, you're getting your comeuppance."

At that moment I hated her and the smirk on her face. I wished I was the type of man who could slap it off; instead I used my words.

"Carlotta, you were too old to have more babies. You were past forty, your eggs were a long time passed their expiration date, and I didn't want to raise a retard. Old mothers have fucked-up babies. Face it: you were too old."

She sucked on the straw sticking out of her Diet Coke can, raised her eyes upward, batted her false lashes—her brows were Botoxed in place so they didn't move—and said, "You think you're so smart. Is that genius mind of yours going to get you out of this mess? I don't think so. Comeuppance!" She turned on her heel and walked out of the room.

"Hey!" I made a step toward her and stopped. She batted her long lashes real slow, and waited for me to speak.

"Forgot to mention. I had genetic tests done on Piper and Milo, like you told me not to do. Said you thought they could have slave blood. Well, they don't. I know the real reason. Obviously, you picked a guy about five foot eight, with blue eyes and blond hair. Was it a sport fuck with your trainer or a stranger?"

"I don't know what you're talking about. Sounds like that cancer has already gone to your big brain." She gave me one of her long looks and turned to go into the bedroom.

"Admit it." I walked toward her, keeping my eyes hard on hers. She flinched. "You went to a fertility clinic after Piper was born. They told you your eggs were old and gave you the option of embryonic adoption. You gave them a piece of my DNA along with yours. They created a male embryo and inserted it into your uterus; you managed to carry the baby to term. Milo's not yours any more than he is mine."

What I didn't tell Carlotta was this theory came from Moma, and I thought it fit. The daughter of a friend of hers had this procedure when her husband refused to give her any sperm when she wanted a third child and he didn't. She was the bread winner, so she bought what she wanted. The kid looked like her other two children. Her husband didn't leave her but stayed because he thought he had an obligation to protect his real children from their crazy mother, but he raised the boy like his own. I saw the wisdom in hanging around for the kids. Besides, divorce was financially and emotionally expensive. I decided to do the stand-up thing until Milo went to college.

I am good at throwing out bait, but she wasn't going to rise to it today. Carlotta simply stared at me for few seconds before slowly pointing to her own head. "Like I said, cancer," and walked away.

I decided to have a beer or two instead of an evening bike ride. I walked down to my pool and called WP, my attorney and friend. I needed a new estate plan, one that would let me control my hard-earned money after I died. I would make sure my widow could not betray my kids or other family members by spending her way to the poorhouse. I wanted a big, fat carrot, a stick, and a noose for Carlotta to hang herself with. I laid back in the recliner and designed her future. It took my mind off cancer.

My cousin, Max Walker, had his attorney draw up a rule-from-the-grave estate plan when he found out about his bladder cancer. I called Aunt Izzy and had her send me a copy of his trust. I would teach my widow the meaning of comeuppance.

I was following the same path as Max. We grew up like brothers, he was less than a year older than me and we were alike in a lot of ways, down to the same type of women we married.

CHAPTER 2 — MITCH STONE

I sat around my saline pool until it got dark. I didn't want to go near my wife.I listened to country music and hoped by setting my thoughts free a grand plan would bubble up from my unconscious. Instead, my mind floated down the river of he past.

I looked at my house. It was a fifty-year-old, well-built home. I liked the floor plan and the feel of the past in it. I added more fieldstone to the outside, raised the ceilings in the living area to a barrel vault, and created a safe haven for my two young teenage girls. They were the only good thing that came out of my second marriage. The three of us picked out a big, cozy sofa, two fat lounge chairs with colorful flowered upholstery, a giant television. The girls decorated their own bedrooms. I taught them the old-style cooking I learned from Mom and Dad.

We had been in the house almost two years before Carlotta entered our lives. She seemed to fit right in and was the right size, almost five feet and about a hundred pounds. My girls were from my second marriage and they were going to be small women like their mom.

My first wife was a giant compared to the second and third. At five foot four, with the curves and tits to go along with it, she was sexy. I was twenty when I got married to her. We'd been dating for a year when she got pregnant. I told her I wouldn't marry her unless she had an abortion, which she did. After a couple of years we got tired of each other and split but we're still friendly. She's a massage therapist now and on her fifth husband.

Carlotta seemed to be a no-stress kind of woman compared to my second wife, Amber, my girls' mother. She is six years younger than me and claimed she didn't want children—mine were perfect for her. We got married less than a year later—and not long after that the unravelling began.

My new wife didn't like the floral designs on the chairs, or the overstuffed sofa, so she bought new ones and sent the others to the Goodwill. All the new furniture was sleek and beige. The color scheme on the walls didn't suit her, so she had them painted soft white. It didn't look like my home anymore but something out of a decorating magazine or a house staged to sell. Carlotta was a Realtor when we met. She showed one of her friends a rental house I had for sale and that's how I met her

Carlotta got pregnant right after we married but didn't tell me. One morning I rolled over and reached out for her in the bed and my hand fell on a cold wet spot. I jumped thinking she'd wet the bed. She took Ambien and slept like she was dead. If a fire alarm went off, she wouldn't hear it.

The light was on in the bathroom, the door open, and I saw a trail of blood leading to the toilet where she sat, elbows on her knees, looking between her legs.

I turned on the bedside light. It looked like a massacre took place on the expensive sheets. At least they could be bleached.

"Are you okay? You look a little white." I called out as I got out of the bed and reached for my bathrobe. "That looks like a badass period to me."

"Shut the door and get out of here. It's nothing for you to worry about. I'm fine but," Her head dropped to her chest and I thought she was going to hit the floor.

"I'm taking you to the ER. You look like you're bleeding to death."

"No!" She held up her hand palm out. "Sometimes I have these really bad periods with all the clots and stuff. Go back to bed."

"Okay. I'll call 9-1-1.That'll be better. I don't want you bleeding all over my new car." I tried to make my voice sound light but I was worried, I made the call, while she was yelling, "Put the damn phone down." I wrapped a blanket around her and listened for the ambulance.

Five hours later we were on our way back home. "Carlotta why are you so upset? I don't get it. We don't want kids, remember. Part of our deal." It was a shock when the doctor told me she had a miscarriage.

She started crying, "I didn't know I was pregnant. I'm on the pill."

"Pills! I've never seen you take pills except

Ambien. You said you had an implant."

"I do, yeah. I'm so upset I can't think. I used to take them. I guess the implant slipped or something."

"The doctor said you were over three months along. How could you not know?"

"I've always been irregular. Just quit talking." She kept her head turned toward the window for the rest of the ride home. It sounded like she was crying, but I didn't try to comfort her with words or touching her. We didn't speak again until I pulled up in our driveway and I let her out. I thought about walking to the house with her but didn't. I was annoyed with answers that didn't make since. I needed to get back to the office. We were working up a bid for a highway job that I expected would make me a lot of money.

"Go get some rest. I'll call later." Something felt off and I wanted to know what. I called a doctor buddy of mine, we ride together, gave him the scoop; he said he'd look into it.

My friend, I call him Dexter because he is a Pathologist, told me a couple of days later while we were on a ride over the Big Dam Bridge. "This didn't come from me—your wife didn't have an implant or take birth control. She's been seeing an Ob-Gyn for this pregnancy. She's even had an ultrasound. Did you know she had a miscarriage a couple of weeks before you married her? She wasn't on any birth control then either."

I was glad we were riding and he couldn't see the look of shock of my face. A previous miscarriage! I didn't know anything about that either. I wondered what else I didn't know about her.

I laughed and said, "I guess I better have a vasectomy."

Dad had one and the recovery wasn't easy as he thought it would be. I didn't have time in my life for healing so I decided I would abstain or use a condom—right.

"You might think about letting her have a baby. Obviously, she wants one."

"She said her doctor put her on birth control the other day to help regulate her hormones, or something like."

"Buddy, you might not know your wife as well as you think." He laughed, "Join the club."

"She is my third one. That says it all—not a good reader of women." I sped up and we raced against each other for the next fifteen miles.

I didn't confront Carlotta, didn't want the drama, I was so caught up in my work that I barely saw her. I'd leave before sunrise and come home just before it got dark so I could ride with my friends. All I cared about was my highway project.

^^^^^^

Four months passed by in a flash. I'd been flying my helicopter, using it to check on one of my highway jobs, and decided to come home early. I wanted to go on a long ride and then meet up with my girls for a trail hike at Pinnacle. I pulled into the entrance to my property. The driveway is circular and extra wide. Being a road contractor has a lot of advantages and my drive was spectacular. I'd built a couple more like it for my buddies.

Amber's car was parked with the trunk open and I noticed boxes in the back. I heard yelling coming from the side entrance and she came running out in my direction. My ex-wife isn't a big woman but she is strong and agile, being a gymnast since she was a kid and teaching in her own gymnastic school. She was past forty and could flip around like a kid. I lent her the money to start her own business and we'd gotten along fairly well after a real nasty divorce.

I walked down the stone path toward the kitchen door and she came flying out screaming, "You fucking asshole." Next thing I knew she'd kicked me in the balls. I'd been the recipient of the move before. I shoved her backward and she hit the ground on her butt but she bounced right back up using one of her gymnastic moves. I stepped backward. Her next move would be a slap to my face.

"Amber! Stop!" I grabbed her arm and pulled it behind her back. "Settle down."

Shelly started screaming, “You are a liar. You lied to me.” I could barely understand her words. Like her mother, Shelly was a drama queen while her sister, Lindsey, fifteen months older, was stoic, and rarely showed emotion. She reminded me of a spider, hanging from a web, waiting to snare her prey. She walked past us, saying nothing, and leaned against the side of the car. Carlotta was no where in sight but she was home. Her car was in the garage.

“Shut up the crying and quit the yelling.” How many times had I say that, probably thousands, over the years Amber and I were married. “What’s wrong? Anyone want to tell me?”

Shelly’s words shocked me. “You said you wouldn’t have any more kids-that we are all you need, but you are having a baby with her and kicking us out.” Snot ran out of her nose and spit sprayed in the air as she yelled.

“What?” I looked at her mother. “What’s going on? Don’t yell it. Say it.”

“Carlotta called, told me to come over, said she had something important that you wanted her to tell me.”

I jumped when my oldest daughter spoke. “Carlotta told Mom that she was pregnant and that you didn’t want us coming here longer. We were supposed to be out of our rooms before you got home.”

Amber couldn’t wait to say, “You are an ass doing this to your girls. They’ll never recover from this betrayal. Coward! You didn't have the guts to tell them yourself."

"I can't believe Carlotta would say something like that."

"You are calling us liars. You're picking her over us."

"No, I'm not. I'm going inside and get to the bottom of this."

"We're leaving, and …."

Shelly interrupted her mother, "You kicked us out!" I opened my arms for my girls to come to me. "There's been some mistake. Leave you stuff here. I'll take it back inside. Go home with your mom and I will figure out what's happened. I'll come over there soon as I can." My girls came to me and we did our group hug, but I felt something had broken between us.I ran into the house calling Carlotta's name but she didn't answer. I found her sitting by the pool, texting.

"What the fuck! You're pregnant!"

"That you hadn't noticed, for the second time, tells me a lot about you."

Her cell rang and she looked down at the caller ID. I grabbed it out of her hand and tossed it in the pool. Carlotta didn't flinch. "I need a new one anyway, thanks."

"The girls said you told them I kicked them out."

"Sounds like Shelly. She's like her mother—needs therapy. I didn't say that."

"Quit stringing me along."

"The other day, I was at the doctor. I got to talking to one of the other women. We're the same age, both around three or four months along, and discovered we knew some of the same people including Amber. I guess that's how she found out, you know, gossip, and she told your girls."

"Why didn't you tell me you were pregnant? Did you think I wouldn't find out until you delivered it."

"Because you would force me to have an abortion, and I want a baby, Now, It's too late to kill it. I don't feel like we are a team anymore. I feel alone. I love the girls being here. We have fun. I didn't do this. Amber did." She raised out of the lawn chair and began to walk away.

None of this made any sense.I felt my temper rise to a dangerous level.I tried to keep my voice neutral but it was impossible. I was shaking with anger."Why would Amber make a story like this up? She's not stupid.There's nothing for her to gain by making me her enemy." I grabbed Carlotta by the elbow. She stopped. Unlike Amber, she didn't hit; she stood still and batted her eyelashes and waited a beat before she spoke in a voice that sounds a lot like a hiss.

"She has that bi-polar disorder and probably not taking her meds. Maybe Amber's trying to break us up and get you back."

I sat down on the chair and put my head in my hands. The whole business of marriage was exhausting."Mitch," she stood over me now. I looked at Carlotta and waited. She had one more thing to say. "The question is, why did Lindsay and Shelly believe that you wanted to kick them out? That tells me there is a trust issue between you and them." She smiled, shrugged her shoulders, and walked off. I shouted, "I'm going for a ride. Go get a new phone." I rode for two hours processing the chaos, trying to figure out who to believe, so I chose to believe my wife. She was pregnant, and it looked like I had deliberately broken my promise to my girls and they were mad and wanted to punish me by moving out.

I went by Amber's and had a talk with Lindsay and Shelly."I didn't know Carlotta was pregnant but I can't do anything about it. I think it will be best to let things cool down. Let's get together on week-ends for a while and see how it goes."

"Daddy, I'm never going back over to your house. I don't even want to see you anymore." That's all Lindsay had to say before she walked out of the kitchen and into her bedroom.

Shelly stood and looked at me and when I touched her shoulder she shrugged me off. "You picked her over us."

Amber had to put in her two cents, "Mitch, we had some real good times and bad ones, but I never figured you would do what you just did. You have a real mean streak. Time for you to ride on back home." She opened the front door and gestured for me to get out.

I was mad at the girls for deserting me and went so far as to remove them from my will. Carlotta wanted that, and I did it to prove we were a couple. I accepted she wanted a baby and started looking forward what I hoped would be a boy. I knew a lot of men my age with teenage children who had divorced and started second families.

Eventually, I patched things up with Shelly and Lindsay, but our relationship never fully recovered. They didn't spend another night at the house after that and when we got together, it was for hiking, or dinner, or week-end camping trips, but no living in the same house.

^^^^^^

A couple of months later, another event happened that I regret. I have a lot of regrets, now that I think about it and Daddy was one of them. He lived about forty minutes out of town. When he was diagnosed with kidney cancer, I wanted him to stay at my house during his treatment. Carlotta said that was a wonderful idea, and Dad settled into the girls' old space. The arrangement didn't last long. I came home from work three weeks later to find Dad gone. Carlotta said he decided to go live on his house boat

"Did he leave a note and just drive off or what? Strange, he didn't call and tell me his plans, don't you think? Did you all fight?"

"He felt good enough to load up his car and leave. I was just coming back from some shopping when he was pulling out of the drive. He told me he was going to live on the boat."

"That doesn't sound like Dad. What happened?"

"Why are you sounding so mean? Your dad wanted to go live on his boat. You're acting like I did something to him."

I didn't answer. I left the house and drove down to the marina. Dad had bought the house boat about the same time I married Carlotta. He had a plan to navigate the rivers and meander to the gulf. It was an older boat he had refinished and brought up to date and decked out with the latest navigational devices. He was sitting on the deck drinking a beer when I walked up. He looked tired, maybe it was the weight loss. He was probably down to one hundred ninety. Dad said he was surprised to see me and told me to get a beer and take a seat.

I got one out of the cooler,"What happened out at the house?

"This morning I went for a treatment. When I got

back, all my stuff was packed up and sitting by the kitchen door. I went down to my room and the bed was stripped and the maid was cleaning the room with some strong smelling disinfectant. I went back up stairs looking for your wife and she was standing at the top of the steps. I asked why my stuff was packed up. She said that you wanted me gone. That it wasn't healthy for her being pregnant and live in the house with someone taking chemo. She said not to blame her that it was your decision not hers. She says you rented a condo for me and the maid could pack up my car if I didn't feel like it."

"That is a lie. I like coming home and seeing you there. It's like when we lived out in the country and built the cabin. Us drinking beer and talking about work. I miss you being at the office, everyone else does too."

"I didn't know what to think after what happened with the girls a while back and I didn't want to cause trouble, so I left." He chugged his beer down and leaned over to get another one.

It was then that I knew for sure that my wife had lied to me—not my girls. Dad was telling the truth. The words, "One drop of water at a time," came into my mind. Carlotta once said that when you are trying to get someone to do something they don't want to do, remember the wicker basket: *It won't hold water if you just pour it in. But if you put the water in one drop at a time, the wicker will gradually accept it and then the basket will hold water. It's like that with people. You can change their lives without them noticing until it's too late for them to change it back.*

Drop by drop, Carlotta got rid of my dad and my kids. What's that saying? Forgive and forget. I may forgive, but I never forget. And I haven't forgotten that. Remembering makes me more determined to tighten the noose that I figured one day would come into play

I found my eyes looking at what I think of as an example of unnecessary excess. I wish I hadn't bought the house next door, which shared our drive, but Carlotta wanted it so she could personally select the people who would buy it from us. The place was priced to sell, the doctor who owned it had already moved to Florida, it was a good investment, and so on and on. I bought it with company money, but Carlotta insisted I put it in both our names. I told her I did, but I lied.

After Daddy died and the girls left, I wanted Moma to stay at my house when she was in town. She usually came with my older sister Birdie and they bunked downstairs in the girls's old rooms. They made dinner every night, ones like we had as kids—fried chicken, fried okra, mashed potatoes, turnip greens cooked in pork fat, black-eyed peas— all that country cooking I loved and missed. My wife didn't cook. Her idea of dinner was take-out.

Moma and Birdie visited two weeks a couple of times a year. They would babysit the kids and picked them up after school, did fun things with them, and the kids loved it. One summer, Moma came by herself. She'd been there less than a week when I got a call at work.

“Mitch, Carlotta just told me you don’t want me to stay at your place next time I come back.”

“You don't believe that, do you?"

"Hell no! Just wanted you to know I won't be here when you get home. I going out to Izzy’s. I can’t be here. It’s not good—not healthy. Let her think she ran me off. I won’t stay in your house with all that hate directed at me.”

I didn’t say a word to Carlotta when I got home except to say, “Where’s Moma?”

My wife said, “Your mom wanted to stay with her sister for a few days, that’s all.” I drove out to Aunt Izzy’s place and the three of us had a talk, and I found out what happened and then I asked Moma to come back after a few days passed but she refused. Next time she came to Little Rock, she stayed with her sister. Then I decided that Moma and I should buy a condo together and she could stay there and so could my girls when they were home from college.

I made the mistake of telling Carlotta about our joint purchase and she hit the roof. She said Moma was trying to put a wedge between us. To prove I loved her and we were a tight couple, I did put the condo in both of our names, showed her the deed, and then had to persuade Moma to stay there; she did but wasn’t comfortable. Now that I think about it, and I wonder why I hadn’t before. Carlotta is totally greedy and destructive.

Then the property next door came up for sale and I sold the condo.

I planned to upgrade the next-door house and sell it quickly, but that didn't happen. Carlotta turned it into what I now call The Playhouse and it became the place my family stayed when they visited. Shelly was living in San Francisco and Lindsay was in New York. It wasn't lost on me that they had gotten as far away from me as they could and still live on the US mainland.

My eyes shifted to the left, and I remembered my plans to build myself a personal retreat over the garage. I was sick of stepping over dog shit on the patio to get into the house and tired of looking at the stacks of this and that lining the walls of all five bedrooms and overflowing into the downstairs.

When I walked down the hall to the master bedroom, I felt like I was navigating a narrow, habitat trail. Piper and Milo's closets, dressers, and bookshelves are loaded with stuff they've had since they were born. The living room and kitchen areas are the only rooms free of clutter. I call them the showrooms. As long as visitors don't go outside these areas, no one has any idea that one day this house might be on a hoarding show.

One day, I boxed up all the extra stuff in Piper's and Milo's rooms and put the twenty boxes in the garage. After I went to work the next day, Carlotta had the maid put it all back. I worry about a fire, and sometimes I think I hear rats and raccoons in the walls at night. I should have the house inspected.

I showed Moma the design for my safe space. I guess the term now days is “man cave.” She wasn’t impressed.

“Don’t kid yourself. What you need is a marriage counselor, or maybe a divorce, but not another room for Carlotta to take over and fill with clutter.”

Moma always says what was on her mind, and on this day, I was smart enough to keep my mouth shut and not defend myself.

CHAPTER 3 — MITCH STONE

I started the cancer treatments a month after my diagnosis. My primary care doctor got me hooked up with Nadir Kamat, a specialist at MD Anderson Cancer Center. He had the cutting-edge cure, was doing a clinical study, and said that my cancer would be a perfect for it.

Carlotta insisted on going to MD Anderson with me, and that was fine. I hadn't spent much time with her since we got married. Most of my time was spent working, creating my companies, and making my fortune. She recorded on her phone everything the physician said. When I asked her why, she said it was to help her understand what was going on. After a couple of trips, Carlotta quit coming along.

I was glad to spend the time alone, no interruptions, thinking about my estate plan. I binged watched *Game of Thrones*, a luxury I didn't usually have. I took a private jet service that made regular trips from Little Rock to Houston and Dallas and carried ten passengers. Usually, I spent five hours at the center and got back to Little Rock in the late afternoon with a piss bag strapped to my leg. Pulling the tube out of my penis was creepy. Carlotta liked to watch which was even creepier. She wanted to do it herself, but I couldn't go that far and shut down the peep show the third time she asked.

The treatment consisted of filling my bladder with

a solution that contained the TB bacteria, which supposedly ate up the cancer. I thought about having my bladder removed but I didn't want to wear a piss bag the rest of my life. I investigated a surgery that constructed a new bladder from part of the intestine but my doctor told me not to even think about that option—the cancer was contained and curable and I wanted to believe him, and the science, but underneath it all, I felt doomed. I was now living what happened to Max.

I was convinced the upcoming Labor Day weekend at Lake Quachita would be my last. I invited Moma and my sister, Birdie, to come along, and I texted Carlotta and let her know. She preferred texts over conversation—she rarely answered her cell. If I wanted to talk to her, I texted first and told her to answer my call. My wife is not quick in a conversation. She listens, says just enough, and then comes back later after she's processed the information. Texts give her the distance she needs to think. That's just one reason she doesn't want to spend time with me, Moma, and Birdie. When we are all together, she can't keep up with the back and forth of ideas and quick retorts.

Instead of going to the office as usual after my treatment, I went home. The week-end at the lake was on my mind, and all I wanted to do was relax and hoped Carlotta wouldn't be around. She usually wasn't that time of day.

As I pulled into our drive, I saw Carlotta loading up the Mercedes Sprinter van, getting it ready for the drive to the lake the next morning. She'd never put a weekend together without my help but for some reason had decided to take charge this time. Carlotta usually drove the kids to the lake and I flew up later in my helicopter, but I wasn't flying now because of the cancer. A licensed pilot can only legally fly if his health certificate is current, and mine wasn't.

I inspected the van, and saw the disaster waiting to happen.Carlotta had managed to wedge some boogie boards and a wakeboard between the racks on top of the van but didn't realize they would fly off if not tied down. I pointed this out and she didn't like it and started to argue.

"Well, those racks up there should hold them on. That's what they are supposed to do. They don't need straps."

I didn't waste my breath explaining how that wouldn't work. I opened the double doors to the back of the van and showed her exactly why the arrangement of supplies and toys she was hauling would tumble on the kids the first hard turn she made. I said ,"Wait until morning and I'll help do it." She huffed and let out a puff of air; she needed a breath mint. "I want that thing packed and ready to go right now. I'm going to ZaZa's and pick up pizza for dinner, so you finish it. You don't look sick to me." I didn't want to argue and kept my voice nice but I didn't feel that way, "Get bungee cords and I'll show you what do."

Just as I finished saying it, Moma walked over

but backed away a step or two when she heard the tenor of the discussion and saw Carlotta stomp her foot before turning toward the garage. I put my arm around her shoulders and hugged her. "I don't want to go to the lake and bounce around in the boat, but I never do anyway."

"You've got the perfect excuse to stay home. Let's sit down over there—you look beat." We walked toward the wooden bench under a big Oak.

"To spite me, she'd go anyway and I'm afraid for her to drive our kids or anyone else's around in the boat or pull them on wakeboards. She might run it up on the shore or over a kid in the water."

After Milo was born, Carlotta wanted the kids to have the lake experience, and I needed to spend time with my family, so I'd gone along with it for the last eight years.That's what a stand-up guy does for his family. Now I'm wondering if this was another of my rationalizations, just a way of doing what I don't want to do and making myself feel OK about it.

We'd been sitting about ten minutes when we saw Carlotta walking back toward the van carrying a load of cords and straps. She waited for us to get back to the van and when we did, she nodded at my mother, then she dropped her load of bungees on the ground in front of me.

"Here's what you wanted." She touched the pile with the toe of her Nike and gave me her little smirk, daring me to bend and pick them up or humble myself and ask her to pick them up for me.

I waited—held her gaze. I just knew Moma wanted to slap Carlotta across what she thought of as a cruel face hidden under a mask of head-tilting innocence. It was a mean act to dare a sick man to perform for her. I saw what Moma was thinking on her face. She stepped forward. I put out my hand and said, "Moma. Don't. Leave them."

I bent and picked up the straps needed to secure the boards and immediately felt a deep cramping in my lower back and a zip of pain streak across my bladder, but I kept my face from showing it. Carlotta looked at Moma and smiled, twisting her long hair around a finger, as was her habit. She walked off with a little extra wiggle in slim hips.

The bungee moment seared into my mind like a brand, as I knew it was burned into Moma's. That incident was the spark that fanned even hotter the fire of my desire to totally control Carlotta from my grave. My plan would look like a stand-up guy taking care of his widow, but in fact it would be total revenge. Max would approve.

Carlotta got in her SUV and drove to pick up supper. She didn't cook—it was takeout every night unless I put something on the grill. I needed to sit down before my legs went out from under me and walked toward the bench with Moma just as a police car pulled up. I walked toward the patrol car as he parked. The officer identified himself saying he needed to follow up on an incident regarding a minor. I had no clue what he was talking about. He handed me a copy of the police report.

Two officers made contact with Carlotta Stone about an incident involving her daughter, Piper. Mrs. Stone reported she was hanging up party lights at approximately 2230 to 2300 when she noticed her neighbor, Rob Riley, had ahold of her daughter by the back of her neck and was escorting her down their driveway while holding a gun in his hand. Mrs. Stone reported the incident frightened Piper to the point that she urinated on herself. Mrs. Stone stated that Piper was going to toilet paper a friend's house and had mistaken Mr. Riley's house for it. While Piper was papering Mr. Riley's house, Mrs. Stone stated this was when Mr. Riley escorted Piper home with a gun. Mrs. Stone stated that when she noticed Mr. Riley in the driveway with the gun, she told him to let her daughter go, and at first Mr. Riley did not. Mrs. Stone stated that Mr.Riley eventually let her daughter go and mumbled something about cleaning up the toilet paper. Mrs. Stone was unable to describe the gun other than stating it was big. Officers were advised that Mr. Riley is an avid hunter. Officers went to his home to make contact with Mr.Riley and noticed the toilet paper in the trees and Froot Loops cereal and crackers thrown on Mr. Riley's porch in front of his door . . . .

"So why are you here? I don't understand." I had to force myself to concentrate. All I wanted to do was relax and not fight another enemy today.

"Sir, an hour after this incident at your home, we

got another call. One of the officers who responded to the first incident responded to this one. It came from a caller who communicated that a female was driving a four-wheeler east on Markham with three kids on the back that were not restrained and about to fall off. The caller followed behind the vehicle to the location of an ice cream shop and provided the address."

He waited for questions or some response from me, but when I didn't speak he continued.

"The officer stayed by the parked vehicle for the driver to return. They spoke with Carlotta Stone, who advised that she had driven their street-legal dune buggy to get some shave ice. She stated all children were restrained. The children appeared unharmed. Prior to leaving the shop, the officer witnessed the children being secured and escorted Mrs. Stone back to her house."

"Why is this second thing even an issue?"

"According to the initial report, the children were not restrained, and a call from a second party reported the same. Sir, I am following up due to the fact that the minor Piper Stone was reportedly involved in two potentially dangerous incidents within an hour of each occurrence."

Cops make me uncomfortable, and when encountering one, I usually keep quiet and act polite. Like Moma, my mouth tends to overload my ass, that's what Daddy used to say. I said I'd talk to my wife and showed my concern.

"There is one more thing. This morning Mrs. Stone was cited for careless and prohibited driving. Two minor children, Milo Stone and Piper Stone, were in the vehicle at the time. Keeping minors safe is a priority with the department. This third incident involving a parent putting her minor children in dangerous situations could result in social services checking on their welfare."

I went cold at the mention of social services. Something felt off about the whole thing. After the cop left, Moma and I walked toward The Playhouse. I didn't want to be outside when Carlotta returned. I needed time to think.

"Moma, I'm not sure how I'm going to handle this, I think Riley just fired a shot over my bow. I bet he followed Carlotta when he saw her load the kids into the buggy and made that anonymous call, and then had his wife make the second one. He probably got one of his cop buddies to stop Carlotta this morning. I bet the one who was just here was the same guy."

"Why didn't she tell you about Piper? She must have known you'd find out."

"I think she was setting up Riley. He's a gun nut, a hunter, a former prosecutor, now he works for the Faraday Firm. I doubt he picked up that gun to scare Piper. I bet he was cleaning it when he saw her messing up his yard with the toilet paper. Carlotta knew he would react when he saw what was happening and had her phone in her hand, calling the cops and recording the whole thing as soon as he walked up. She's hoping she can file charges against him, or plans to threaten him.

She didn't tell me what happened because I would put a stop to it. Riley isn't the kind of person you want as an enemy."

I knew I looked tired but wired at the same time. I couldn't shut up and kept on talking about Riley and Carlotta. "They've been feuding over the smallest of things since he moved here. She had that house in mind for one of her friends and he upped his offer and got it. That started it. She probably put Piper up to that toilet paper stunt because he's having a dinner party tonight and he is particular about his place. Carlotta had another run-in with him the other day about the kids riding their bikes along the edge of his lawn and mashing the grass. Get this, a couple of weeks ago, Piper poured superglue in the shape of a big heart and sprinkled glitter over the glue on the street in front of his driveway. Carlotta knew about that and didn't punish her."

"Sounds like Riley's at the top of her grudge list."

"I'm betting first place belongs to you. Don't let her pull you around on a wakeboard this weekend. She'll make you fall off and run over you when she goes back to pick you up. I'm not kidding."

"She's that diabolical?"

"Yes, she is. When she looks at you she sees me and that says it all. Watch your back."

CHAPTER 4 — MITCH STONE

The Corp of Engineers created Lake Quachita in the fifties by clearing land, building a dam, and flooding areas that once were towns, homes, roads, a cemetery, and a field that produced a fourteen-pound sweet potato and it won first prize at the state fair. Trees still stand upright in parts of the lake and their tops show when the water drops low enough.

Motels and cabins sprouted along the shorelines. Shangri-La was built on the east-facing shore, and all the rooms looked out on the sunrise, which reflected in the water. The restaurant became famous for its homemade pies. Everyone who worked there seemed to be related. The McSwain clan discovered it in the early sixties, and it became their place to go on long weekends.

I hate Shangri-La. The owners had never upgraded anything since it was built sixty years ago. That is part of the charm, I was told. After a night's sleep, my back told me the mattress and box springs were the originals, and that didn't feel charming to me. I wanted to stay at the lodge on the other end of the lake. It had a great restaurant, hot tubs, a spa, the works. But Shangri-La was Carlotta's family's summer tradition and her mother was treated like royalty by the owners. They remembered Carlotta's dad, and that went a long way with the McSwains. I couldn't stand spending time with the bunch of them. At night they set up charcoal grills in front of their rooms and cooked hamburgers or steaks and served pies they bought in the restaurant. My attendance at the evening meal was expected, maybe required, but I went along.

My older sister, Birdie, rode in the Sprinter van with Carlotta, the kids, and her sister's two children, who were a few years older than Piper and Milo. Moma and I rode up later, spending our time in the car talking about my Grand Plan. Right now it was in the developmental stage, and I enjoyed tossing ideas back and forth for discussion with Moma, who should have been a lawyer instead of a historian. I liked the way she thought, but I had to mature into it. As a boy, her thinking scared me.

I remembered back when I was twelve and she was married to Harvey Beck. I wrote her a note saying I wanted to live with Dad because, "I don't like the way you think." She picked up the phone, called him, and said, "Mitch doesn't want to live with me. Says he doesn't like how I think. So instead of waiting until he's fourteen, come get him now."

Dad came and I left with him. Moma was cut and dried that way. It took me a long time before I realized I'm that way myself, and by the time I was twenty and married for the first time, I realized I wanted her in my life. There was no discussion; we just got back on track. Maybe because she got sick and the doctors told us Moma was going to die, but she made it.

Moma and I got to Shangri-La around suppertime. Birdie and Moma went to the lodge for dinner and I did the usual thing with the McSwain clan. The next morning, Moma, Birdie, and I met for breakfast and sat down at a table for six at the motel's restaurant. We were the first customers in the place. Moma brought a small container of organic cream and set it on the table front of her. She ordered two egg whites cooked crispy, Birdie got eggs scrambled, and I had the wake-up special, which included lots of bacon.

Carlotta's sister, JoAnne, walked in with her mother and they chose to sit at another table. The sister came over to our table to explain they were waiting on her kids and husband and a couple of his nephews. She looked down at the table and spotted the cream.

"Where'd you get that?" It was more of a demand than a question. JoAnne doesn't look a bit like Carlotta; she is tall, a beauty contest winner in her youth, and a lawyer married to a lawyer.

Moma said, "I brought it,"

JoAnne reached down and put her hand around the container. "I want that. They don't have real cream here, not even half and half."

Moma grabbed JoAnne's wrist and held it. "Leave it. We don't have enough for everyone."

JoAnne made a huffing sound and said, "I'll bring it back after I use it."

"You might want it, but you can't have it, so put it down." She gave JoAnne's hand a little jerk.

I said, "Moma, let her use it."

"No, if I had been asked, I might have, but I

brought this. She's been coming here for years; if real cream was important to her, she would have brought some herself. See it for what it is, Mitch—a power play. She's saying, 'I can take what I want and you won't stop me,' and she's saying that to you, not me." It seemed like all the oxygen had been sucked from the room. JoAnne huffed off, and I said, "Moma, why did you do that?"

"You pay the way for more than your wife. Has anyone in that family every thanked you for all the things you've done for them? I don't think so. You told me JoAnne and her husband come up here all the time when you aren't here, take out your boat, and never even put gas in it. Carlotta's mother speaks to you like you're her employee and you take it from her. If I treated you like that, you would be all over my ass. What do these people have over you?"

Birdie didn't like this kind of talk and said, "OK, OK. I see both sides. Let's just eat and get out of here."

After breakfast, the three of us went for a walk along a trail following the shoreline and all seemed forgotten. Birdie and Moma drove to the lodge across the lake and went to a yoga class, had lunch, bought some T-shirts with blissful sayings on them. When they got back to Shangri-La, I was sitting on the patio in front of their room, drinking a beer, looking out at the lake.

"I let Carlotta's mom have it. I got to thinking how you called me on it and you were right. I made her cry.

She's such an uptight bitch, I didn't think she had tears in her. I told her exactly what I knew about her supposed wealth, the money she owes on that farmland, and I wasn't going to pay it off when she died. I figured Carlotta would want me to save the farm for Piper and Milo, but I'm not going to. I said everything I've thought, and it felt good. I guess people with cancer do that sort of thing."

Birdie and Mom knew better than to say a thing. I opened a couple of beers and we sat around and drank them and waited for the sunset.

When I got up the next morning, Carlotta and the kids were not in the room. I guessed they were at breakfast. I went to Birdie and Moma's room. Birdie had just finished her shower when I walked in and handed her a cup of coffee. I took the cream out of the small beer cooler and said, "Thought we could start the morning without drama."

Birdie said she thought I was out on the boat with the kids and Moma. She said, "Piper was here a little while ago, and Moma went along when she said you were down at the dock, waiting."

I panicked. "Holy shit! Let's go."

At the end of the day, after a couple of beers, I read what Moma had written in her journal about the shit show that had played out.

Piper came knocking on the door around eight this morning. She wanted me and Birdie to go wakeboarding with them. Birdie wasn't up, but I said OK and told Piper I would meet them at the boat in about ten minutes. I supposed

JoAnne and her two kids would be with them, but it was only Carlotta, Milo and Piper.I asked where Mitch was, and Carlotta said he was running a little late. After about fifteen minutes, Carlotta texted Mitch and said he wasn't feeling good, but he wanted us to on without him.

I looked at the sky and the water, as was my habit, living in Maui and windsurfing and swimming in the Pacific. I asked Carlotta, "Do you usually wakeboard in this much chop? Look at the sky. There is a lot of wind up there." Carlotta said, "We do it all the time like this. Are you scared of the water?" I said, "I'm surprised you would take the kids out in these conditions."

I stepped onto the boat, and Carlotta backed it out, scraping the sides as she maneuvered out of the slip. She headed out into the open water as the boat banged against the chop. She stopped the boat in a large cove and Piper set up the wakeboard.

Piper said, "You go first, Gran. First is best." I asked Piper to explain what to do, because I'd never done this before, and she showed me how to position my body and my feet. I put on my wetsuit vest and got into the chilly water. On the first pull, I flipped. Piper and Milo got a good laugh at that. The second time I made it, and the ride began.

Carlotta went full throttle ahead, made several soft turns, and we flew down the lake. It was thrilling and scary at the same time. I saw a guy puttering around the edges of the lake on his jet ski, and then it seemed like he was following us. We were the only boat on the water. I saw Carlotta was heading in the direction of the shallow end of the lake. If Carlotta turned in the wrong cove at that speed, I could be slapped face-first into one of the treetops above the water. I hoped she would just keep going straight down the middle of the lake, but she didn't.

She *cut hard, bringing the boat into a small cove, and I almost fell. At first I thought she was trying to make me fall, but considering it was Carlotta, and Mitch said she wasn't a good boat driver, I told myself it was inexperience. Then she headed toward the end of the cove. I saw treetops sticking up. I realized I was going to hit and let go of the rope short of impact with the tops and swam toward them and ducked down.*

Carlotta suddenly turned the boat in the other direction and headed toward the open water. Then she made a sharp turn and headed back toward me at hight speed. The boat was bounding out of the water. Suddenly the guy on the jet ski was next to me, holding out his arm, He said, "Get on. If that boat don't turn soon, it's gonna hit you." He pulled me to shore. It was close enough that I could have back stroked to the shore but I was reluctant to make even a short swim into the open water. I was afraid she would run over me, like Mitch said.

He pulled the jet ski next to the bank, and we watched Mitch's boat bouncing high in the chop toward the treetops. It looked to me like Carlotta tried to make a hard U-turn to avoid hitting them, but it was too late and the boat too far out of her control. It skidded into the branches, tossing Milo out. He landed hard and didn't move. The jet ski man was on him in seconds and snatched him up and brought him to me.

Milo wasn't breathing. The guy said he'd been a paramedic in the army and knew what to do. He gave Milo CPR and then Milo threw up water and started to breath. He took off his T-shirt and wrapped Milo's arm close to his body. "I think its broken, but don't worry. It's gonna be fine. I'm calling 9-1-1, and they will get to the dock before we do."

He told me to get on behind him and hold on to Milo; he would take it slow and get us back to the dock in one piece. Mitch's boat idled next to the treetops. He yelled out to Carlotta, "Are you OK? Can you drive?" Carlotta looked like a crazy woman She yelled for him to put Milo down or she would have him charged with kidnapping.

He took a picture of her and Piper and told her he would send someone out to help. Carlotta headed back to the dock in a hurry, speeding past the jet ski, creating a wake that rocked us. I held Milo tight but could feel him slipping. I squeezed him tighter and wondered if Carlotta was creating the wake on purpose.

When we got back, there was an ambulance waiting, and Birdie and Mitch were standing there with a crowd of people. Carlotta pulled into the slip so fast she took off a corner of the dock and made a dent in the boat. When I saw the look on Mitch's face, I knew shit was gonna hit the fan. All I wanted to do was get back to the room, take a shower, *get away from Shangri-La for the rest of the day. Beer wasn't going to be enough recovery drink—unless it is accompanied by a shot or two of tequila—**It for now.***

As soon as I heard Moma was in the boat with Carlotta, Birdie and I ran to the dock. My boat was gone. JoAnne's husband was standing there. He said that he was supposed to go out with them and asked me, "Where'd they go?"

"I just found out they were gone."

About that time, an ambulance pulled up, along with a deputy sheriff who said there had been an accident on the water and the victim was being brought in by jet ski. I asked if it was a kid and he said it was.

Carlotta came in hot and slammed into the side of the dock. The jet ski with Moma and Milo on it was a safe distance behind her, and the driver eased in an empty slip and the paramedic carried Milo to the ambulance. He was pale and a T-shirt was holding his arm to his side. Carlotta started screaming. "That man ran us down. He took Milo from me. Arrest him."

I stepped forward. "Carlotta, shut up! Get out of the boat. Go to the room. Keep your stupid mouth closed. Piper, you go with Birdie. I'll handle this."

The paramedics examined Milo and prepared to take him to the hospital. They thought his arm was broken.

"I'm going with him," Carlotta screamed and ran toward the paramedic. I stepped in front of her and grabbed her by the upper arm, pulled her close to me, squeezing her harder than I needed to. "I told you to go to the room. Do it. Get yourself under control."

JoAnne's husband stepped forward, put his arm around Carlotta, and walked away with her.

"Moma, I want you and Birdie to take Piper and go into Hot Springs and find something fun to do. Wait there for me to call." I started walking with them to the room.

Moma stopped. "I feel like this is my fault. I should have listened to your warning. I just couldn't back down and . . ."

"I know. Believe me, I know. Now, go take care of my girl so I won't worry about her."

"OK, I'll get my stuff." She walked back to the boat, reached in got her beach bag, and I saw her pick up Carlotta's phone. She brought it to me. "Your wife didn't text you earlier. This whole mess was a setup."

By late afternoon, I was back at Shangri-La with Milo, his broken arm set and in a sling.

The next day, I sold my big-ass boat to the man who saved Milo's life. He bought it for a hundred bucks. A good deal for both of us.

CHAPTER 5 — LEE EDWARDS

I was flying low over the Arkansas River n my chopper on my way back from Memphis when the call came from Jim Worth, a Little Rock attorney. I didn't answer. I was enjoying my ride low over the fast moving water. I had done several jobs for Worth and didn't like the man much.

I think of Worth as a little man, but not because of his small stature. It went deeper than that. Worth came from an old Little Rock family of bankers and had the entitled ways I despise.

When I returned the call, Worth said, "Lee I'd like you to meet the daughter of an old family friend. Her daughter really needs your help. It's Carlotta McSwain Stone, the McSwains from down Lonoke way. Her husband, Mitch, is in a serious medical situat on in the hospital. His mother is coming to town, and that's a problem for her."

I didn't tell him I knew Mitch Stone. I didn't mention that I'd started my PI business after I retired from military service and that one of my first clients was Mitch's father. He suspected his second wife was having an affair with the married carpenter who was redoing their kitchen. I provided him with the proof.

The first job I did for Mitch, his dad recommended me, was when he suspected his second wife, Amber, the mother of his two girls, was sleeping with the yard boy, and I confirmed it. When Mitch suspected his controller was stealing, I was the one to crack open the case. When I needed financing to start my other businesses, Mitch loaned me the money, but I didn't tell Worth that either.

"What's the problem? Why does she need an investigator?"

"I'm just making introductions, helping her mother; she's worried about Carlotta, nothing to do with the law. To be frank, I'm not really sure, but she asked me to find her daughter an investigator, and you're the best. These kind of people only want top-choice, if you know what I mean."

I agreed to meet Carlotta Stone the following day. After Worth's call, I pulled up the Pulaski Clerk website to review the current cases he had in Circuit Court.

I found two open ones involving Mitch Stone's mother, Elle Hawk, as defendant. Jim Worth represented the plaintiffs, Harvey Beck's three daughters. Hawk was the trustee of the Beck family trust. She was married for thirty-two years to Beck, but they had no children together. Elle Hawk was the primary beneficiary. Beck had a no-contest clause in his trust. The sisters were challenging her—they'd lost twice already.These lawsuits followed one after the other, and Worth represented each of Beck's daughters. Considering Worth's filings against Elle Hawk, the claim he wasn't representing Carlotta, but helping a family friend, caused my bullshit meter to rise.

I arranged to meet Carlotta at Joyce's over on Washington in North Little Rock. The trailer, shaped like a block building, served soul food on Styrofoam plates. It was hardly a place I expected Carlotta Stone would know about, but she had selected our meeting place.

I was vaguely familiar with the current Mrs. Stone, having worked for Mitch over the years. Once, I saw him at Kroger in the checkout line with a dozen boxes of Zone bars and a case of Diet Coke and a pack of straws. He said his wife subsisted on Zone Bars and Diet Coke to keep her weight down, and it was now the diet his young daughter had adopted. You can imagine that I was surprised when Carlotta Stone suggested Joyce's, and even more surprised to see her inhale the chicken fried steak covered in white gravy, collard greens with specks of ham, mac and cheese, a side of cucumbers and onions, and three corn muffins slathered in honey butter.

I finished up my green salad topped with blackened catfish fingers. After wiping my mouth and hands with a paper napkin, I carefully refolded it and placed it to the side of my styrofoam plate, and recapped the Tabasco bottle, lining it up with the salt, pepper, and ketchup. I intentionally waited to ask Carlotta why she had requested this meeting so she could enjoy her food and relax. I knew it was important for Carlotta to feel comfortable around me, which she clearly was, given how much food she'd just eaten. I expected she would pull over her husband's supercharged Cadillac and throw up her lunch. But right now, she looked extremely satisfied.

I groom myself in such a way as to make my white clients feel safe and to inspire trust. My grandmother had told me I could thank her for my light complexion and white features. I wear my salt-and-pepper hair cut close, so there's absolutely no hint of curl. I don't really need the expensive round glasses but feel they gave me a slightly professorial look and make my lean, muscular physique less edgy. I select various wardrobe pieces from Stitch Fix, which keeps me on trend with pieces not found in the local mall. I supplement those with shirts and slacks I pick up on my travels to Dallas and New York. My fashion conscious clients recognize the effort I put into my sartorial choices. Clothes are my *obvious* indulgence.

After Carlotta finished her meal I opened the conversation. "Jim Worth didn't give me a heads-up, so I have no idea what I can do for you." I sat back and waited for her to fill me in. Carlotta looked up through her long, false eyelashes, chin down as she took one last drink from the straw in her can of Diet Coke. I waited and would wait as long as it took or until I decided this meeting wasn't worth satisfying my curiosity.

When I first meet a potential client, especially a woman, I try not to prejudge based on their various social and economic factors. I accept who she is without judgment, especially in today's environment. Mrs. Stone came across as studied, from the way she dressed, to her table manners, to her soft-spoken, almost breathy speech. My first thought was that she was trying to imitate Jackie Kennedy.

When I first started out in the private investigation business, I wouldn't have considered working for a white woman like Carlotta Stone, more stubborn than sensible, who had managed to hook a man like Mitch Stone. I sensed she was trouble with a capital T, but nothing in her manner told me that except that it was studied.

Finally she answered my question, but her words and the meekness of her manner didn't match. "Lee, I'm looking for someone who can set a trap and catch a rat for me," She waited for me to say something but I kept quiet and she went on a rant about Elle Hawk. "She told Mitch to make an estate plan that would ruin my life after he died; she was always driving wedges between us; she is mean and she is a liar." The tirade went on for fifteen minutes.

Mrs. Stone reminded me of the Yellow Eyelash Viper, a tiny, yellow snake with extra scales over its eyes that makes it look like it has eyelashes. I first encountered one in Costa Rica. I was hiking with a guide, and there was a gate we had to open to go into the forest reserve. I reached for the rope that held the gate to the post, and the guide grabbed my hand just in time. If he hadn't, I would have touched the viper, which was curled on the wooden post. It's a beautiful little thing that's extremely poisonous. The viper didn't stir; it stayed curled up like a jewel waiting.

What was Worth thinking giving this crazy woman my name? I work for a lot of high-profile people in Arkansas and across the South, from Dallas to Atlanta. Very few people are aware just how far my reach goes, and I want it to stay that way. Spying depends on discretion, and this woman who tried to look discreet was probably just the opposite.

Before I decided if I would work for Carlotta Stone, I wanted to see for myself what kind of condition Mitch was in. I went over to the hospital after visiting hours. Mitch was alone, sitting up in bed watching television when I opened the door and knocked before I came in. He put his index finger up to his lips and showed me the palm of his hand. I got the message, nodded, and closed the door.

When he came out into the hall, he looked fine to me except when we walked to a small waiting area, he was unsteady on his feet. We sat down and he told me about his bladder cancer, and that he'd had a small stroke and expected more strokes to come. "Lee, I'm surprised to see you. What's up?"

"Well, for starters, I'm wondering why we are sitting out here and not in your room."

"You go first and don't go all discreet on me. It's got to be big or you wouldn't be here. I might look fine to you but I could stroke out at any minute—not kidding—dead man walking."

I told him about Worth and my meet and greet with Carlotta.

Mitch said, "I drove myself to the emergency room a couple of days ago. It's a long story I won't go into right now. I need to get to the point. My first night here, I left my cell and laptop on the stand next to my bed. The next morning they were gone. I was about to call for the nurse but one of my accountants walked in. I used his phone and called Carlotta. She said she was afraid they would get stolen and took them home. I asked her to bring them right away but she didn't show up until that afternoon and when she did, she brought my cell but not my laptop. She brought a new one with her, said she had it programed to play my favorite songs, and set it open on the night stand."

He needed a break from the talking and took a few deep breaths, "She is stupid to think I couldn't see what was going on; laptop is streaming video to her. She didn't bring mine back until the next day. I discovered she hacked into it and now she knows my plans about the trusts I've set up. I've been keeping that to myself. I wouldn't be surprised she is sitting out in the parking lot right now watching the room wondering where I am and will walk in here."

"What do you want me to do about working for her—yes, no— how can I help? All you've done for me. I owe you."

"Let her think you are her man. You still use the same bank account for transfers?"

I nodded yes and was about to ask Mitch what he had in mind when one of the nurses came toward us. She said, "Mr Stone, your wife called the nurses station and asked if you were okay—said you weren't answering your cell and asked where you were."

Mitch told her he would call his wife. "See, she gave herself away. I bet she's on her way over here so you better head out—take the stairs. I'll get in touch tomorrow. Oh, and Lee, I will make this worth it for you to stay on her until my kids are grown. Tomorrow, check your balance. A dead man walking feels generous."

I took the stairs and ducked into the coffee shop next to the entrance. I'd just taken a seat when I saw Carlotta Stone cross the entrance and run to the elevators in her high heels wearing tight black slacks and a black top with her dyed blond hair hanging free and flowing past her shoulders.

CHAPTER 6— ELLE HAWK

I'd gone back to Little Rock four times since Mitch was diagnosed and began his treatment, but this visit would turn out to be the hardest one on me—on all of us. He'd been declared cancer-free in March, but in less than a month our world fell apart.

According to Birdie, Mitch had driven himself to SVI Emergency room feeling dizzy. Carlotta didn't arrive until two hours after he called her, but his attorney, WP Kelpe, came right away. Then he called Birdie and told her what was going on. When Carlotta got there, several physicians explained what they found—multiple hemorrhagic infarcts on his brain MRI. She refused to believe them.

The doctors said to WP they were unsure if she wasn't capable of understanding or was too upset to think. Carlotta told WP she didn't know any of the physicians at SVI and didn't want Mitch admitted there. She called a friend of hers who was the wife of the chief of staff in one of the departments at the University of Arkansas Medical Science Hospital, or maybe it was the medical director, WP didn't know, but he thought Carlotta wanted contact with a bigwig that would give her connections. Arrangements were made and Mitch was transferred—against medical advice—to the UAMS hospital, about a mile down the street. I arrived the afternoon Mitch was admitted to the medical school hospital.

I'm seventy years old, but I don't know it until I look in the mirror. I don't pull an overstuffed roller bag, I wear a red backpack. I don't walk or dress like an old woman. I love boot-cut Levi's and tie-dyed shirts, and hiking boots. But I don't wear those things often because I live in Maui, so most of the time I'm wearing beach clothes. I keep my gray hair cut short like a Catholic schoolboy.

I learned the art of getting old gracefully from my second husband, Harvey Beck. He was seventeen years older than me and an inspiration. His words of wisdom for aging—always walk with purpose; keep the stride long; the back straight; your language current; never complain or talk about your aches and pains.

I picked up the rental cal and drove out to Whole Foods. I like to make my own food and I picked up several bags of fresh greens, vegetables, fruits, eggs, and Ezekiel bread, then drove to Heights Liquor and bought a case of Duvel beer, before making my way to Mitch's compound on Broadview Drive.

The Playhouse served as a place for our family to stay when in town, but its primary purpose was a home for the children's hobbies. Carlotta turned the main living room into a dance studio for Piper, with mirrored walls, bars, a gymnastics floor, sound system, while the upstairs den was for Milo's Judo . I was surprised to see that two pet rabbits roamed free in the attached garage that led to the kitchen. It smelled and looked like the rabbit droppings hadn't been cleaned up for a long time. Carlotta wasn't home when I got there.

I spent most days at the hospital with my daughters and grand daughters in Mitch's room. His speech was a little slow and he walked off kilter but he communicated fine. When we were alone, he filled me in on Lee Edwards and their deal. I often went back at night and slept upright in a chair. Edwards had placed monitoring devices in Mitch's hospital room. No one said or did anything that wasn't observed or heard. Carlotta, not Mitch, wanted this surveillance, but Mitch thought it could work against her.

A couple of days after I arrived, Carlotta said she needed personal protection and Mitch told her to call Apollo, he said she likes to think of herself as a Kardashian, but didn't tell her Lee owned it. Apollo posted a guard twenty-four hours a day at the entrance of the compound and another one to follow her around when she thought she needed it—she wanted a big bruiser type to protect her.

The team at UAMS put Mitch through the gauntlet of testing and found that he had, among other problems, a tumor in the pulmonary vein that extended into his heart. The physicians tried to contact Kamat, Mitch's cancer doctor at MD Anderson, several times to discuss his condition, but neither Kamat nor anyone from MD Anderson would return their calls. It became clear, MD Anderson wanted nothing to do with Mitch, and that puzzled the Arkansas physicians. They talked to me about it because I had his health care proxy.

UAMS surgeons refused to operate on Mitch to

remove the tumor, saying it was too risky, there was a good chance he would die, and even if the mass was removed, it was too late. There were too many tiny tumors traveling through his body and taking hold in his brain and elsewhere. Mitch, who was able to comprehend, indicated that he wanted the tumor removed. I asked him why, and he said, "I want to die on the operating table. I can't take any more of this."

Carlotta called some more of her friends who were married to doctors and got the name of a highly respected surgeon. Ironically, he worked out of St. Vincent, and suddenly the hospital that wasn't good enough was the place to be. Paperwork was signed and Mitchell was transferred back to SVI and underwent an embolectomy with Dr. Frank Bowen, aka the "cowboy surgeon."

Bowen was the son and grandson of prominent Little Rock surgeons, and he wanted to perform this difficult and delicate surgery, an operation he had only performed once before. If he succeeded without killing the patient, it would be another big win for him. Removal wouldn't cure the cancer, but that wasn't his problem, and this patient understood that. Bowen was Mitch's kind of man, one who wasn't afraid to take the chance. What made the case even more rare for Bowen was that Mitch was the cousin of Max Walker, the patient he'd performed the embolectomy on a few years earlier.

Mitch wanted me with him in the ambulance on his return to SVI. Once he was installed in the transport, he told me to listen and not ask any questions. It seemed I was always being told *don't ask questions*.

"This is probably the last time we'll have any privacy. I told you Carlotta is spying on me. Trust Lee—he's a good man. Been day dreaming about what's probably going to happen when I can't think clear any longer or when I'm dead. Carlotta will find an attorney from a high-end firm, a really smart young lawyer, a man of course, who will tell her what she wants to hear and he'll take her down the road of challenging my trust. The attorney will help put the noose around her neck and not realize it—until it's too late." Mitch laughed and looked like his old self for a minute or two. "She'll get even with him too—count on it. But they won't beat me and my plan."

I didn't speak or ask questions. I sat and held his hand and tried not to cry. The transport pulled into SVI. It was the beginning of the end of our time together on this earth. Mitch squeezed my hand and said, "I love you, Moma. Be careful."

Three days later, the cowboy surgeon did his magic. It turned out the tumor Bowen removed was metastatic. Pathology returned consistent with high-grade urothelial carcinoma in both this tumor and the adjacent lymph nodes. Mitch had a bladder tumor in his heart, just like his cousin Max. With every heart beat, cancer cells travelled his body.

When Mitch was discharged from SVI after his epic operation, he made it clear to the physician who discharged him that he wanted “quality over quantity.” He didn’t want chemotherapy or more hospitalizations; his primary goal was to go home and be comfortable. I was there to support his decision. Carlotta was not. She wanted him to live, because as long as he was alive, and able to think, Mitch’s trust would not come into play.

Mitch went home with hospice arrangements in place and twenty-four-seven private nursing care arranged. Carlotta refused to hear the words “hospice” or “cancer,” and was opposed to hospice coming to her house. She wanted only private-duty nurses, but Mitch said hospice worked for him. So he ended up with both.

Carlotta wasn’t available to bring him home. His good friend Troy drove Mitch’s Cadillac sports car to the hospital to fetch him. It was the same car Mitch had driven to the ER. At that visit, the neurologist told WP Kelpe, “When I met Mitchell Stone, I could not believe I was looking at the right patient. It should be impossible for a man with his MRI to walk straight, much less drive a car, but the patient had done just that—amazing.” That’s the kind of man Mitch was. Yes, *was*. He would never drive his sports car or fly his helicopter again.

Carlotta stubbornly refused to believe any of the things the physicians told her. She chose to think the Arkansas doctors were wrong and insisted on taking him back to MD Anderson for a second opinion. But no one from the cancer center would return her calls, and she was angry. While Carlotta was threatening lawsuits against MD Anderson, my daughters, his girls, and I tried to make his journey to the other side comfortable.

Edwards remotely monitored the comings and goings of every individual going into The Playhouse, the main house and its sick room, den, and downstairs area. He watched the first shit show hit the fan.

Before dawn one morning, I walked next door, spoke to the guard, and went into the healing room expecting to find Scott, the registered nurse, at his post next to Mitch's bed.

As I entered the room, I heard Mitch's soft, shaky voice. "Moma, is that you?"

I took his hand and sat on the edge of bed. "Where's Scott? Isn't he supposed to be on duty for two more hours?"

"Don't know. I need help. Have to pee. I had an accident." He started to cry. "My whole body hurts. My legs are cramping bad."

I went to the stand where his medications were arranged. I looked at the list, which showed he was over ten hours late on his narcotic medication for pain and on the muscle relaxants. The pill bottles were gone. I went back to his side.

"The meds are gone. The nurse is gone. I'm going to get Carlotta."

"No, that'll cause trouble. Get me to the bathroom."

I tried to help Mitch get into the wheelchair, take him to the toilet, but with his cramping and his weight, I couldn't. I needed Scott for that. From trying to help Mitch sit up, I realized he was wet and cold and his bed was soaked in foul-smelling urine. The pads used to protect him were gone—again. I knew he was humiliated: he kept his clothes and his body cleaner than normal people and had since he was a kid. He was reduced to pissing on himself and sleeping in it.

It dawned on me the pee pads had become a symbol of the power fight between me and Carlotta. My mind went back to the day after Mitch came home from SVI after his operation—the day the pee pad war began.

Carlotta stood in the doorway of the bathroom while the nurse's aide finished helping Mitch with his shower. The aide was explaining to him that incontinence protection was essential. I listened as he recommended waterproof pads to protect him and the mattress; incontinence was a hygiene and a comfort problem. I was sitting in the healing room, reading the latest Jack Reacher novel on my Kindle.

The bathroom room suddenly erupted. Carlotta screamed at the aide, "Those damn adult diapers will make him lazy. He needs to get up out of bed. He needs the work. If a man pisses on himself, he deserves to lay in it. If you put a diaper on him, don't come back. I mean it." Carlotta gave the floor a stomp with her foot and walked out. I made the mistake of trying to reason with her.

After a near accident an hour later, I put several waterproof pads under Mitch. When I came back, the pads were gone. Day after day, the battle of the pads went on without either of us saying anything about it to the other.

On this morning—the morning of the missing night nurse and the missing pain medication—I realized the battle of the pads was a continuation of the tug-of-war between me and Carlotta that began in the waiting room after Mitch's tumor removal. I thought about the intense scene when the surgeon gave us his report.

I can still see Dr. Bowen when he walked into the post-surgery waiting room after the five-hour operation. He was tall, bald, and looked fit and strong. I had Mitch's health care proxy, so Bowen directed his words to me. Carlotta didn't seem to comprehend what he was saying anyway. She kept interrupting him with senseless questions, asking him to spell a word and wait while she Googled it. He grew impatient, ignored her, and made his report to me. I saw from the look on her face Carlotta felt marginalized, disrespected, and it made her angry. She walked away and sat down next to her mother and sister. She had a big support system there—cousins, friends, some of Mitch's employees—all crowded in the waiting room watching the surgeon and me in a deep discussion. Carlotta wouldn't forget the humiliation.

I brought my mind out of the past and concentrated on the job at hand. I needed to get Mitch to the bathroom but I wasn't big enough to handle him. I said I was going to get Birdie to help but Mitch told me to find Scott. I ran downstairs to the space that years earlier had been where Mitch's daughters stayed during the alternate weeks they lived with him. Then Carlotta got pregnant with Piper and kicked them out.

I knew the whole scene was on video and would be watched by Lee Edwards and Carlotta would ask to see it. I opened the bedroom door to the left. It was empty. Then I went to the right and opened the door. The nurse who was supposed to tend my son was in the bed asleep, snoring. I pulled the covers off him, exposing his entire nude body, and gave him a hard shake. He jerked awake.

I stood over him. "Get up. Get dressed. Get upstairs. Do your fuckin' job!"

Scott couldn't reach the covers and tried to cover his penis with his hands. He said, "Carlotta said I could take time off. Sleep here. I have a full-time job at the hospital. I'm tired. I need rest. I don't need to sit beside him the whole time."

His resemblance to Mitch was uncanny, and I wondered if that was why Carlotta hired him. I ordered him to "Get upstairs. If you can't do your job, you'll be replaced."

I jumped when I heard the words, "You can't tell Scott what to do. I pay him. He's on my team." Carlotta said it in her signature slow hiss.

I turned and faced Carlotta. Got up in her face. "So, you're OK with Mitch suffering extreme pain? That's what you want? Oh, and the humiliation of sleeping in his own piss. You want that for him too? Yep, I can see you do."

"Scott is my employee; he'll do what I say. You don't have any power as long as Mitch can still think for himself."

"You're wrong about that."

Scott, with his hands covering his private parts, got out of the bed. I stepped forward and kept him from opening the bathroom door, then demanded he give me the pain medication.

"I was told he didn't need it. I don't have it," he whined. He had the blond hair, and blue eyes of Mitch, but he was a coward.

"What doctor told you that? You're a registered nurse. You work at SVI in critical care. You know better. Be careful about making medical decisions on your own. You might endanger a patient."

"Don't you threaten me. Carlotta told me what you are. You're probably drunk or high on pot right now. You're a threat to everyone. That's why all that security is around here, because of you."

"Is that right? Well, I suggest we both get drug-tested. But in the meantime, put on your panties and get back to work."

When I turned to leave the room, Carlotta, who

had been capturing it all on her cell, stepped aside and let me pass. She and Scott stayed in the bedroom. I went back upstairs, called the guard into the house, and asked for his help. He said it wasn't his job and went back outside.

"Mitch, I woke Scott up. He should be up here any minute.Something feels off with that nurse."

Mitch took a few deep, slow breaths. His legs were twitching with cramps. "Get down close so you can hear me. I pretend to sleep so I can listen. They're trying to set you up. I want you to talk to Lee and . . ." He didn't finish his thought. Scott was standing behind me.

"Hey, Mitch, let's get you up. I was on a break. Carlotta said you needed me." Scott put Mitch in the wheelchair and pushed him to the toilet and changed him into dry pajamas. He asked Carlotta for clean sheets, she refused, so he helped Mitch get in to the bed on the dry side and gave him some Extra Strength Tylenol. Carlotta told me to get out. I refused.

The nursing aide came at seven, gave Mitch a shower, dressed him, put him into the wheelchair while he changed the bed. The babysitter came, fed the kids breakfast, and took them to school. The housekeeper arrived and began cleaning the kitchen and started laundry. Carlotta left the house and was soon replaced by her mother, two of her women friends. Her sister, JoAnne arrived with a female security agent from Apollo.

I called WP about the missing medication and asked for advice. He said it would all probably sort itself out, that I should be calm. He did nothing to help Mitch. That wasn't what I wanted to hear, and that was when my distrust of him started. WP didn't even sound upset, and that made me mad at him. I called hospice and asked them what I could do. Then I contacted adult protective services and found out the protocol when an infirm adult was in danger.

In the meantime, Birdie and her husband, Mark, had come in and found themselves in the middle of the mayhem. JoAnne was trying to strong-arm me out of the house. I said I wouldn't leave until Mitch got his medicine. Mark intervened and tried to calm things down. JoAnne said she didn't know where Carlotta was or the medication.

I punched in the APS number on my cell and shoved the phone in JoAnne's face. JoAnne is six inches taller and thirty pounds heavier than I am, but she retreated as I advanced. She tumbled over an ottoman and landed hard on her back, hitting her head on the floor.

She stood up and screamed, "You pushed me. I could have broken my neck. You're dangerous. I'll have you arrested for assault."

"I didn't touch you. You backed up. It's not my fault you don't have spatial awareness. Get the medication within five minutes or I *will* call 9-1-1 and tell them Mitch is having a heart attack."

I explained to JoAnne's audience what would happen if I called emergency and an ambulance arrived. It would be best for Carlotta to get Mitch's medication.

JoAnne said she would see if she could locate Carlotta, left the room, returned, said Carlotta was now taking phone calls. JoAnne tried to negotiate with me about giving her more time. She told everyone that her sister was traumatized by the atmosphere I had created in her home.

I said, "Well, isn't that too bad? Too much talk and no medicine will result in the call. The clock is running. You've got about two more minutes, JoAnne."

She turned toward Mark. "Please, one more try. Maybe Mark can help reason with Carlotta. Can you give us a few more minutes?"

Mark nodded that he would help, and JoAnne asked him to join her in the next room. I thought she wanted to get a feel for Mark, thought he might be sympathetic to Carlotta, and she wondered how he felt about me.

Later, Birdie told me that Mark told her not to play chicken with me, that I would take it over the edge. He said that was how I worked.

JoAnne returned to the room with the medicine but refused to give it to me. She addressed the room like she would jurors in a trial.

"Carlotta will only allow me to give the medicine to Mark, and he will give it to Scott. Although Carlotta still maintains the narcotics are keeping Mitch from healing; she fears what his mother will do if she doesn't give up the medication."

JoAnne thanked Mark for helping Carlotta "during this difficult time." She touched his shoulder. "I especially appreciate his insights and warnings about Elle Hawk and I pray peace can be restored here."

I clapped my hands and said, "That sounds like a closing argument to me. You should quit being a debt collection lawyer and go into trial work." I looked around the room. "You could use the video from all these hidden cameras to build your case against me." I swept my hand around to indicate where they were, and to create a diversion, which got the attention of JoAnne. I plucked the phone from her hand and put it in my pocket. She grabbled at me and missed.

"All of you make me sick. This is about a dying man, not his wife." I left the room and went to Mitch. I heard Mark tell JoAnne he would get the phone from me and suggested everyone calm down.

I transferred all the data from JoAnne's cell to another device and set it on the table, where the meds were supposed to be. I would point to it when Mark came in to save the day. Later that day, Birdie played a conversation she'd overheard between JoAnne and Carlotta and recorded it.

"Carlotta honey, I hope I've finally earned your trust. Hiding that medication pushed Elle Hawk right over the edge after that long tug-of war over the pee pads, just like I thought it would. She doesn't have a clue what she's up against." "She is just like Mitch

They are always thinking they're the smartest people in the room. Maybe a few more crazy outbursts will sink her." "Right. She will be neutralized, and that job as trust protector will disappear. When we go to court to have Mitch's health care proxy revoked, she won't have any more power." "Come to think of it JoAnne, you can do more trust building. "What do you need?" "Sweep up that mess of rabbits turds out in the garage."

That night, I came back to Mitch's room to say good night. I got to the doorway but stopped when I saw Carlotta crawl into bed next to him and toss one leg over his midsection, looping her arm over his chest. She snuggled close, pushing her pelvis into his side ever so slightly, making a small, humping motion with her hips. I couldn't tell if he was awake or asleep; he was wearing one of the masks I put on him because the light bothered him now that his eyesight was reduced to shadows. Mitch didn't flop around as much as he had before he wore the eye masks. He couldn't sit up without help; in fact, he couldn't do anything without help.

I watched as Carlotta slipped her hand under the waistband of his warmup pants, only to encounter the Depends. She pulled down his pants and ripped them off. I heard her say, "If you can't control your bladder, you deserve to sleep in pee." Carlotta got back on top of him and pulled the sheet over both of them. "I'm not going to let you go; you know that, don't you?" She whispered other words I couldn't hear as she continued to work to get a reaction from what I assume was his penis. Carlotta rode him like they were having sex. I saw her lean down close to his ear, her long hair falling forward, obscuring her face I heard her say, "Shame on you for giving your mother your health care power of attorney. Don't worry, I'm not going to let you escape into death—Sweetie."

I couldn't take it any longer. I already felt creepy spying, but the humiliation she was heaping on Mitch got to me. I came up behind her, grabbed her by the shoulders, and pulled her off of him and tossed her on the floor. I wanted to kick her in the face but kept control.

"I captured your performance on my cell—learned that trick from you. I will either put that on YouTube or I will take it to adult protection services and ask them what to do if you ever denigrate my son again. On second thought, I'll call a lawyer." I dialed JoAnne's number and told her to get over to Mitch's or I would call 9-1-1and say Mitch was having a heart attack, anything to get him out of this house of horrors. I didn't call WP Kelpe; he wouldn't do a thing except tell me to calm down and wait for things to work themselves out. JoAnne was there in five minutes, along with her mother. Carlotta left with them and didn't return until late in the next afternoon.

The shit storm blew over. Scott kept his job, the medications were given as directed, the pee pads were no longer removed. It was as if the whole incident had never happened. It took about two hours, but JoAnne earned more trust by sweeping millions of turds out of the garage.

^^^^^^

Ten days after the pee-pad-missing-medication shit show, I flew back to Maui, Birdie and her younger sister drove back to Cincinnati, and Mitch's daughters went back to the East and West Coasts. MD Anderson Center agreed to see Mitch. Carlotta told everyone involved in his care that she expected him to be admitted and treated. She asked WP to make arrangements: hotel reservations, cars with drivers, a private jet, the works. Carlotta, Nurse Scott, WP, a security agent from Apollo, and the patient boarded the jet and headed down to Houston. The group arrived a day before the appointment so Mitchell could rest and be at his best.

WP called me after the appointment. The visit didn't go as Carlotta planned, The physician who treated Mitch's bladder cancer was not even there. A female physician met with him, Carlotta, and Mitch. Using test results as evidence, the doctor explained why MD Anderson would not admit or treat Mitchell.

"Carlotta acted shocked and got aggressive." Kelpe played the recording he made on his cell of Carlotta's reaction to the physician: *What is that red dot between your eyes. You're probably not a real American. I don't understand why the fucking hell you got us down here if you weren't going to admit him. Why isn't Kamat here today?You are not his real doctor anyway* —it went on and on.

WP said, “Carlotta didn’t look angry, her expression didn’t change, but her words were hostile and disconnected.”

I told him,”Her expression can’t change because of the Botox, and the nips and tucks. He didn’t comment except for, “Oh.”

According to WP, Carlotta stomped her foot and left the room. “I thinks that’s her go-to reaction when she doesn’t get her way.”

That he realized this and said it out loud surprised me. I wondered if he was more observant than I thought.

WP played part of the tape: *Your condition and prognosis were explained to your wife before this visit. I was informed that you knew that you would not be treated or admitted. Due to the constant threats of a lawsuit from your attorney, our legal department suggested this courtesy visit.* The physician handed Mitch a copy of a letter from Jim Worth and MD Anderson’s response, but Mitch didn’t look at it. He said he didn’t know about the threatened lawsuit.

“Elle, I didn’t know anything about Mitch’s wife until he got sick. I’d never spent time with her. Carlotta said we were bringing Mitch to Houston for treatment. It didn’t occur to me that she might be lying.”

“Well, I’m guessing Carlotta thought she could force the doctors to change their minds.”

“When the doctor asked Mitch if he was aware of his prognosis, he nodded yes. She asked if he knew if the visit was just a courtesy? He shook his head no. She asked if he had known, would he have come anyway, and he nodded, yes. She asked why, and he said, 'Wife needs closure.' And that said it all."

WP took a long pause. "We got back on the jet the next day and returned to Little Rock. Mitch had a massive heart attack along the way, and when the jet landed, it was met by an ambulance. He was taken to UAMS. He's in serious condition and I don't know which way it will go. Carlotta filed a petition to challenge Mitch's health care directive and got a restraining order that keeps you from making medical decisions."

"I need to go to that hearing." Kelpe said, not a good idea. He said he heard I would be served at the courthouse.I asked for what and he said, "Remember that service in Maui that was declared invalid? You're going to be served again on that same matter with the Beck Trust and it will happen at the hearing."

If WP was right, this would be Worth's second attempt to have me served in this case. The first try, ironically enough, had occurred the day I arrived back in Hawaii after Mitch's operation.

I thought back on that night. Chris Curtis, a process server in Maui, came after dark. He stumbled into a decorative screen at the foot of the steps going up to my deck and shattered it. This caused my dogs to bark. He made his way up the stairs to my front door. I was lying on a yoga mat in my living room, stretching out in the dark after my long plane ride. The door was closed but not locked. I didn't plan on falling asleep on the floor. When I heard the commotion and the banging on my front door. I stayed put and listened.

I don't open my door to strangers. I learned many years ago what can happen to a woman if she does. A friend of mine opened her door to a deliveryman carrying flowers from a florist shop. He chased her through her house and shot her in the head while she was hiding from him in her bedroom closet. He left the flowers by her body. The card read, "Have a nice day." Her husband found her. That was the Mary Lee Orsini-Yankee Hall murder case, which was a big deal in Little Rock but probably not anyplace else.

When Chris Curtis opened the door to my house and placed the documents on the floor, he broke the rules imposed on process servers. I knew this and called the police the next morning to report what happened. The young officer who came to the house asked me why I hadn't called right away. I said, "I didn't think of it until I talked to my next-door neighbor, who happens to be the assistant to your police chief. She told me that I should report Curtis."

The officer asked if I had a gun, and I said yes, but it was in my bedroom and I couldn't get to it. He asked if I knew that, legally, I couldn't shoot someone outside my door, and I said yes; I'd taken the gun course, as required by Hawaii law. He asked me how I could remain so cool, and I told him about my murdered friend.

A police report was made, Curtis was interviewed, and he told them a different story, saying he had spoken to me and given me the summons. Curtis claimed he'd acted according to the rules, it wasn't dark, he hadn't opened the door, we'd had a conversation. My neighbor's bedroom window faced the stairway up to my front door and she had heard the commotion, looked out her window, and she saw Curtis go up the steps. This went into the report too. I objected to the service, and it was declared invalid.

^^^^^^

I figured Worth knew I would come to Little Rock sooner or later to see my son. Like a sniper, he waited for me. The thought of a process server appearing at the hearing didn't surprise me. Since my husband's death, and the Beck sisters started their lawsuits, I'd been stalked and served eight times. There has been one polite server, and the rest had been assholes. I knew I would be easy pickings this time, essentially in a corral, the server wouldn't have to work for it.

I didn't tell anyone except Doyle, my daughters, and WP Kelpe that I was going to the hearing. When I met with Kelpe, I learned he had hired another attorney to represent me and the health care proxy. I thought that was WP's job as Mitch's attorney, I asked him why and he said if he represented me, or even came to the hearing, it would cause confusion. I didn't get the reasoning and neither did Clarence Doyle. Plus, we couldn't understand why Kelpe thought I would be served at the hearing, unless he was psychic. The temporary attorney and I sat across the aisle from Carlotta and her legal team of four. I wore an indigo shirtwaist dress and she wore a black suit dress, a short black jacket, her hair pulled back in a low twist, and diamond stud earrings. She looked like a Barbie-plays-attorney doll. Her female lawyer took her through a series of questions in which she answered in a soft voice, appearing vulnerable, as she told her lies.

Carlotta told the judge that Mitchell's ability to speak clearly was affected by the stroke, that was true, but "Mitchell is totally mentally alert. He communicates with me in other ways. I ask him questions and he answers by nodding, or he uses one or two-word answers. His thought process is normal."

Her female lead attorney encouraged her to explain. "I asked Mitch if he wanted to stay at UAMS and get cancer treatment, and he said yes, and he nodded yes too. I told his mother that, but It didn't matter to her. She wanted his doctors to withhold food and water and was sticking with that. It didn't matter to her that he was getting well."

Carlotta waited a beat and looked up at the judge. "I've been with Mitch every day and night since he's been diagnosed, and I know better than the doctors or his mother that he is communicating and getting stronger every day. His doctor told me yesterday that all he needs is 'the wind beneath his wings,' and he will get well."

Carlotta didn't mention to the judge Mitch nodded yes to every question. If asked if he wanted medical treatment, he nodded yes. If asked if he would like to eat a shit sandwich for lunch, the nod was yes. She also did not tell the judge she had not seen a head nod in a few days or explain that what she called words were actually grunts Mitch made when she asked a question and then poked at his chest to get a response. I knew these things because Lee Edwards filled me in. Apparently, Carlotta forgot he put cameras in the hospital room.

Two medical specialists from UAMS testified: "Communication is not possible and the patient doesn't have the capacity to make decisions. Mitchell Stone has medical conditions that will cause him to die regardless of whether or not life-sustaining treatment is provided. He could live a week or a month; we don't know. His condition is incurable and cannot be reversed."

WP did not come to the hearing and the judge wanted to know why.,"Where is this WP Kelpe? Why isn't he here? He wrote this document." My attorney said WP another commitment. The hearing adjourned and the crowded gallery filed out. The process server, smelling like old sweat in a dirty, tight-fitting T-shirt barely covering his beer belly, waited for me in the hallway outside the courtroom. He was obviously instructed by Jim Worth to intimidate me.

When I stepped into the crowded hall outside the hearing room, the server came up from behind and pressed himself against my back. I stepped away, turned around, and drew my head back away from his face. He tapped me on the front of my left shoulder with the papers and said, "You've been served."

I gave him a little shove and said, "You stink like yesterday's Bourbon—go take a bath and get out of my face." I know that's not socially acceptable, me shoving him, but neither is him pressing his stinking body against mine.

The server said, "Ma'am, I'm truly sorry to serve you this way." He actually looked like he meant it, but who knows, he probably enjoyed it.

I told that smelly asshole, "If you meant that you wouldn't be standing out here waiting to serve a mother who was in court begging a judge to let her suffering son die."

Doyle stepped between the two of us and guided me toward the exit. He saw my fist ball up, and I think he feared I would strike Davis in his big gut.

Birdie and I went to see Mitch as soon as the hearing was over. When we got there, two of his uncles were with him. It wasn't until then that I realized how important Mitch was to the Stone clan. Within the last two years, they had lost two brothers, a sister, and now they were about to lose Mitch. I felt sorry for this family that was so close to each other. I didn't have that when I was growing up.

WP asked how it went and I told him about my encounter with the server. He pressed his lips together before he said, “I warned you.”

My tone was a little combative, “How did you know he would be there?”

He shrugged, “Makes sense Worth told the server. I warned you.”

“Worth didn’t know I was coming in for the hearing. You told me the process server would find me. Unless the process server or Worth are psychic, how would either of them know I was even in Little Rock? Oh, so you know, the judge wanted to know why you weren’t there.”

The neutral look he usually keeps on his face slipped a little, “It sounds to me like you’re accusing me of something.” If there was a string of trust between us, it snapped when WP looked toward Birdie and Shelly and rolled his palm in their direction. “Maybe it’s someone close to you; ever think about that?” His voice sounded kind, his face looked sympathetic, but his words were cruel. It was destructive for Kelpe to suggest that those closest to me were betraying me.

I walked off toward my daughter and granddaughter. They were talking with a couple of the nurses, who wanted to know about court. The doctors, nurses, aides, the head of the UAMS legal department, everyone involved with Mitch’s care, had come to me during his stay and said they hoped the judge would uphold the health care directive. All stressed that he was suffering and it wasn’t fair. It was cruel.

Twenty-four hours later, the court ruled, "Elle Hawk is authorized to act on her son's behalf in making end-of-life medical decisions for her son consistent with the advanced directive." The temporary restraining order that had kept me from making medical decision for my son was set aside.

Mitch won that battle, but there would be more ahead. It was clear to me that WP Kelpe wouldn't fight for him.

Within three hours of the order, Birdie and I watched as a medical transport team removed Mitch from UAMS and delivered him to SVI Hospice. Carlotta chose not to be present. The last I saw of her, she had stopped by his room before the team arrived. She was all decked out in black tight pants, high heeled shoes, a sparkly top. To me, it looked to me like she was going to a party.

CHAPTER 7 — BIRDIE

Mitch had spent ten days in a private room at UAMS before the judge upheld his health care directive. During that time, I stayed at The Playhouse with Shelly, but Moma chose the Marriott in downtown Little Rock. A couple of days before Mitch was moved to hospice, Shelly and I took a break from our morning with him and went back to where we were staying. It was a sunny day, and we sat outside on the front patio enjoying lunch before going back when we heard a car pull into the driveway at his house.

"Oh good, it's the maid," I announced as I stood on my tiptoes to spy over the hedge at his house. "It's so cold in that hospital, I'm going to borrow a sweatshirt from Mitch before heading back. I guess it's not really borrowed; he won't need it again." I hadn't packed for a long hospital vigil when I left Cincinnati, but that was what it was turning out to be.

"I'm coming too. I'm taking Dad's Rolling Stones T-shirt."

We cut across the lawn. Even though we were heading to the front door, it felt like we were sneaking in. Mitch was never coming back to this house, and as soon as he was dead, Carlotta would kick us out. At this point, we were tolerated. I thought I should get a storage unit and pack up the Stone family mementos and furniture that wouldn't be part of Mitch's estate. It would be a whole lot easier now than later.

The housekeeper left the door unlocked. That

was good; it would seem weird to Shelly to have to ring the doorbell of her father's house. We called out "Hello" as we walked toward the master bedroom. The maid waved to us from the far end of the kitchen.

The house was basically one giant rectangle, with bedrooms coming off two sides. An open stairway going down to a den with two additional bedrooms with baths were on each side of it. Glass doors opened out to the patio and pool area.

I recalled how Carlotta's mother had threatened to call social services if Carlotta didn't put a baby gate at the top of the stairs. Her mother had said she couldn't bond with Piper if her grandchild was in danger of dying by falling down the steps and breaking her neck. She would later repeat that threat about the pool. It needed a fence around it. Carlotta didn't want to destroy the flow by putting up barriers. Mitch agreed with his mother-in-law and the gate and fencing went up.

It was an odd dichotomy in a house, especially one with a maid three days a week. Carlotta's side of the bedroom was filled with an assortment of old magazines, unopened packages, mail, and miscellaneous things, as was the attached media room. Swaths of material covered the clutter. I had seen unopened packages shoved under every couch and bed in the house. When I'd come last spring to watch Piper and Milo while Mitch and Carlotta were on vacation, I'd done a thorough inspection.

Snooping was not my habit, but during that stay I had been locked in the house while Milo nursed a spring cold. I'd lifted up material from a stack between the piano and the wall to discover toys from the past Christmas. For some reason, I looked under a couch and found an assortment of things from picture frames to toys, all still in their original packaging. Soon I found myself looking under every bed and finding stacks of toys, clothes, unopened boxes of plastic plates, and so on. I took pictures of it all and sent them to my mom.

The excess was sickening. Moma and I could not figure out why Mitch put up with it and had spent many hours speculating what Carlotta could have over him. Everything that had to do with him was neat as a pin: his side of the closet, his side of the bathroom, of the master bedroom, of the garage, his car, his office, basically anything he owned that she did not touch.

I riffled through Mitch's sweatshirts, while Shelly grabbed an old jacket with the original Stone company logo and a pair of UGG warmup pants I had given him for Christmas. I figured Moma would like to have those things. Shelly was busy on Carlotta's side, holding up clothes with tags still attached. She shoved a few of them in a backpack that she had grabbed from Mitch's side of the closet, saying, "She'll never miss these."

Shelly hadn't brought enough stuff to stay this long and was sick of wearing the same things over and over. "You wait," she said to me. "Carlotta will see me in one of these and not even recognize it is hers. Basically,

I'm pulling these shirts out of clothes purgatory."

I felt a little weird but understood Shelly felt a lot of anger toward Carlotta, even more than the rest of their family, and I knew taking a few shirts felt like a little win. Plus, I agreed that Carlotta would never notice; they had come from the middle of the racks. There had to be fifteen feet of hanging space on Carlotta's side of the closet, and there simply were too many things for her to notice the few tops Shelly was liberating.

"I think we need to get some boxes and pull out all of our family things from The Playhouse and get it ready to move. You know as soon as your dad is gone, we'll probably have trouble getting our stuff out."

Shelly looked at her phone, checking the time. "Carlotta won't be back for a couple of hours. I'm going downstairs to get my stuff. I boxed it up when I left for college and put it in a closet. I want my yearbooks and things." We set the backpack by the front door and went downstairs.

The maid was busy in the laundry room and paid no attention to us. It had been a while since Shelly had gone into her old room, and she was surprised to find it turned into a LEGO room for Milo. The closet was stuffed with Piper's overflow of too-small clothing and dance costumes.

"Good Lord! Why doesn't she get rid of some of this stuff?" Shelly said as she pulled things out of the way, trying to get to the back of the closet. I stood by the window, looking out over the back patio and pool. It really was a beautiful house and yard. Who knew what it would look like in a year? After just a few weeks, the energy in the house felt different without Mitch. It was like the house knew he was never coming back.

"Shit! My boxes are gone. Seriously, this house is crammed full of crap and my stuff was thrown out. I hate her fucking guts."

"Maybe they're in the other bedroom." We made our way across the toy strewn playroom to Lindsay's former bedroom. It was free of kid clutter. This was now the place Mitch had his weekly massages before this last hospitalization. The table was set up at the foot of the bed. The closet was completely empty except for a white robe and a set of slippers.

Shelly was on the verge of losing it when she remembered the hidden storeroom. Halfway down the steps was a landing. One of the wainscoting panels had a pressure-sensitive hinge that opened to a crawl space that led to a large storage area under the kitchen and laundry room. The space was high enough to walk in upright. Mitch had wanted access underneath the split-level house without having to crawl through dirt.

"I'm hoping Dad moved my stuff here and didn't just toss it."

I felt the wall and found the light switch. We gasped when the light came on. Someone had gone to great expense and trouble to create the miniature, mature oak tree that stood in the middle of the room. Standing six feet high, its branches spread out a several feet in each direction, and on those branches swung miniature bodies.

"What the fuck is that! That tree looks just like the one from her mom's house.Remember that first Easter?" I rubbed the back of my neck, trying to get the hair to stand down.

"That is some sick voodoo shit," Shelly whispered as I creeped forward to get a close look at the bodies hanging from the tree. "It's her lynching tree. That's her hit list! Do you think Dad knows about this sick shit?"

There were at least twenty-miniature dolls resembling humans hanging by their nooses. I took one off the tree to examine it, then carefully rehung it exactly where I'd removed it.I didn't recognize the woman whose likeness had been scanned onto fabric and turned into a doll with a hairstyle made from human hair.We quickly recognized many of the likenesses hanging from the tree, including our own and Mitch. Both of us took out our cell phones and started taking pictures of all the dolls and the tree

"We need to get the hell out of here," Shelly said as she started to remove the doll bearing her likeness of dark brown hair with a blond streak, dressed in blue jeans shorts and a white T-shirt.

I reached out and stopped her. "We can't take any of these. We've got to leave this place just as we found it. Carlotta can't know we were here. If you take your doll, it's the same as announcing you were here. She's clearly crazy. Plus, we can't take ours and leave the others."

It felt like we were under the house for hours, but only twenty minutes had passed. We quickly exited on to the landing and moved the panel back into place. We heard the maid in the master bathroom cleaning as we crept up the stairs. Shelly grabbed the backpack as we ran out the door."My heart is beating so hard, I think I'm going to pass out,"

Shelly said, "Do you think the maid will say anything to Carlotta about us being down there?"

"Nope, she only hires maids who don't speak English, and that's the only language she knows. Carlotta just points, and eventually, she fires them because they don't understand what she wants."

An hour later, when I got back to Mitch's room, the first thing I did was check to make sure Carlotta wasn't holed up in the bathroom, pretending like it was an office so she could listen in on whatever was going on in the room. Creeping was a skill Carlotta had perfected. I pulled up a chair and sat with my bare feet propped next to Mitch's on the bed. I took a photo of our feet. I did this every day he was in the hospital. The quiet of the room was a nice change from the revolving door of well-wishers and gawkers. He had to be in hell, having so many people see him laid bare and vulnerable.

I opened one of my ever-present notebooks and began writing about the tree with the hanging dolls. I shut my eyes and let my mind roam back to the first time I'd seen the real lynching tree. I picked up my pen.

2002. Easter. McSwain Farm ——

I didn't realize this was a semi-family meet and greet —didn't know Mitchell was going to marry her. I'd come to town on the spur of the moment to see Daddy's new boat. Later, I realized lunch was a setup so Carlotta's mom could scope out the future in-laws.

The house where Carlotta's mother lived was a very old, plantation style—white brick—impressive, from a distance. Up close, the wood columns and window facings showed dry rot and needed attention. The house was filled with antique furniture. The rugs were old and worn in places but looked like quality, not something you throw out, but something you repaired.

Mrs. McSwain steered us into the family room attached to the kitchen. It appeared to be the room in which she spent the most time, the furniture selected for comfort, not show, but like the rest, worn. A black woman in a maid's uniform worked on lunch. She announced, "This is Billie. She's been with our family forever. I don't know what I would do without her help in this big old house."

Billie look up, smiled, went back to getting the last of the meal together while McSwain poured drinks. They worked together like an old married couple.Carlotta said, that Billie was part of their family. Lunch was a formal affair in the big dining room served by Billie, who, despite being just like family, ate her lunch alone at the kitchen table. We weren't exactly comfortable.

Seriously, who dresses their help in a uniform in this day and age? We'd expected a cookout, not Billie in the kitchen. Even Daddy was caught off guard.

After lunch, Carlotta took us on a walk around the farm. She wanted to show off where she grew up. At the far end of the property, away from the main road, she stopped under a giant ancient oak and hugged it, saying she just loved this big old tree. It was her favorite on the whole farm. It was the family lynching tree.She petted its bark and looked up at its thick branches.

"Lynching tree?" I asked, thinking I'd heard wrong as I rubbed the goosebumps that suddenly appeared on my arms. Carlotta's eyes gleamed with what I assumed were tears. Now I know it was excitement over the whole idea of being able to lynch a person. She said, "You know, a hangin' tree where they'd hang a nigger who got out of line, or some white trash thief. I'm not saying it's OK to hang people, even the ones who deserve it. But back then, you know, people took care of things on their own. It's not the tree's fault."

I hadn't thought about that strange lunch again until today. The reproduction of the lynching tree and the hanging dolls brought it all back. I know it is some type of hit list, cursing list, revenge list. All I know is that it gives me the total creeps. I'm not sure she's sane. I need to tell someone about this, but who? It's not like she's breaking any laws,

I closed my notebook and looked at my brother. I had put the sleep mask over his eyes because I sensed the bit of light he could see bugged him. "I'm calling Moma on speakerphone so I can tell both of you what Shelly and I saw at your house today. I don't know if you understand or care about Carlotta's shenanigans, but today, we ran across some truly twisted shit at your house."

Moma answered on the first ring. "I was just getting ready to come to the hospital. How is Mitch?"

"Same, I'm with him now and you're on speaker. I've got to tell you what happened this afternoon at his house. It is so truly fucked up. I don't even know what to do about it. I can say for sure there's something wrong with Carlotta."

I described the whole afternoon, from grabbing the sweatshirts to searching for Shelly's boxes to finding the lynching tree, as I now called it. Moma didn't say a word until I finished the whole story. She asked me to send pictures and I did.

While we were on the phone, I said, "Mitch, I'm going to assume you are awake and want to see these photos, so I will pull up your sleep mask and hold the phone in front of your face." I tried to treat him the way I would want to be treated. I wasn't sure if he understood what I'd reported. I knew if he was cognizant, Mitch would want to see the pictures, so I held up the phone and flicked through them ."I'm just trying figure out what to do about it. I don't think Carlotta is stable. I wish I knew what you thought." I squeezed his hand.

At the mention of his name, Mitch became agitated. He moved his head back and forth and squeaked, "Eee—eee—eee."

Moma asked, “Is that Mitch?”

“Yes, I hope the show and tell wasn’t a mistake.”

“You and Shelly need to get out of The Playhouse right now and check in here. I’ll pay for it. I’m hanging up now; be there in fifteen minutes.”

Moma was right. I called Shelly and told her to pack up all her stuff. We were moving to the Marriott.

CHAPTER 8 — NURSE AMY

Mrs. Stone stood with her back against the wall outside the hospice room, right leg bent, foot flat against the wall, texting, waiting. I was at the nurses station waiting too. Her posture reminded me of "the working man stance." It was the way the dishwashers at my family's hotel restaurant often stood when they hung around waiting for the dirty dishes and cutlery to pile up. They assumed that position—leg bent, foot on wall, smoking, not texting.

This fancy woman always wore Lululemon stretch pants, or leggings, not sure what they're called, and tops that matched. She had a habit of twisting a strand of her highlighted hair with her index finger when she talked. She looked high-end, but she stood like a working man—showing the world who she was without opening her mouth. I figured she'd come out of Lonoke County, daughter of a farmer with a lot of land in his family but not much money. I grew up in Little Rock and went to a private school. We called her kind a "country princess."

The soon-to-be widow waited in the hall for her husband to die while his sister was in his room, holding his hand, her eyes closed so her last sight of him wouldn't be watching his final breath and the husk he would quickly become. Usually, there was a line of visitors for him, but this day, in the late afternoon, the hallway outside his room was empty and had been all day.

Mrs. Stone could have gone in his room, even though the day before his mother had given the order that banned her from hospice due to her risk to the patient—she was removing his pain patches. In spite of her cruelty and because she was his wife, I called to let her know her husband's death was a few hours away. I left a message on her cell and texted her, but got no response.

I also called his sister, who arrived within fifteen minutes. When Mrs. Stone did arrive a couple of hours later, she chose to stand in the hall with her foot against the wall and wait for her husband to die.

Mitch Stone arrived here in hospice six days earlier, but to all of us—the doctors and staff—it seemed longer due to the daily drama that surrounded him. There was some sort of family court battle over his advance health directive. The judge upheld it, and within hours, he arrived and was set up in a room close to the entrance of the hospice floor.

Saint Vincent Hospice is on the seventh floor of the main hospital and is open twenty-four-seven to accommodate all who want to visit the dying. On Mitch Stone's first night, around midnight, two big bouncer types came in with his wife and tried to remove him. A member of the floor staff became concerned when he peeked inside the door to check on the patient and saw him slumped in a wheelchair.

Mrs. Stone claimed her husband was restless and these were his two best friends, and they were going to roll him around outside the hospice area to settle him down. The head nurse called security. The wife stomped her foot, said he needed stimulation, threw a minor fit, threatened to call her lawyer. When security arrived and prepared to escort her and the men off the floor, she relented, and the three of them left.

We moved Mitch Stone to an empty room next to the nurses station so he could be watched, and the order came down from his mother that there would be no visitors to his room after 10 p.m. I had never heard of someone trying to kidnap a patient, and neither had anyone else on the staff.

The next morning, another new thing happened. His second wife, that's how she introduced herself to the staff, aided by a friend of hers, hauled in an abundance of framed pictures and hung them on the walls and set them on the window ledge and the nightstand next to his bed. They laid down fancy Oriental rugs to make the place homey and put handmade quilts across his bed. Vases of fresh flowers were set around the room and a rocking chair was brought in. By the time she finished her redecorating, the place looked like a woman's bedroom.

At noon that same day, Mitch Stone's first wife came by. She added that piece of information about herself when she explained to the nurse who she was and what she was doing to Mitch. She said she was a therapist, and that she'd come to give him a massage. She first gave him a sponge bath with lavender oil in it, then she rubbed essential oils into his body, massaged him, put magnets on his body while chanting over him with tuning forks. She also came that evening and chanted. I wasn't sure what magnets did for him, or the tuning forks either, but I could understand the benefit of the massage and maybe the essential oils. She did this every day except this one, his last day to be alive.

On that same day, Mrs Stone set up cameras in the room. When the patient's mother discovered them, she reported it to the head nurse, and security removed them. Mrs. Stone replaced them with an iPad. She told me it was programmed to play his favorite music. His mother took a look at it and said it streamed images into Mrs. Stone's computer, and that way she could watch the room while sitting in her car in the parking lot. His mother took the laptop, stomped the screen until it shattered, and threw it in the janitor's trash can.

During the time Mitch Stone was here, his two sisters, his mother, his friends and business associates, employees, personal trainer, cousins, uncles, aunts, his two young children and their babysitters, his two adult children, created a stream of visitors that flowed out into the hallway. Drama erupted at times between the factions.

On day four, the true shit show went on display to a hallway full of Mitch Stone's visitors. The double doors opened, and a dark-haired girl of about sixteen, obviously a babysitter, entered with his two children. They were followed by their mother and an African

American woman of impressive stature dressed in black slacks and a white, starched, long-sleeved top.

On her way toward his room, Mrs. Stone ducked into a vacant one. I had seen this move before. She often hid in empty rooms close to his and spied on what was going on in the hallway.

Elle Hawk, the patient's mother, saw her grandchildren as they walked through the double doors, followed by their entourage, and walked toward them with her arms open in a greeting. Piper, the older of the two stopped and said in a loud voice, "Stay away from us, Gran! Mom said Dad's here because you are murdering him. You keep away."

That stopped the grandmother in her tracks, but she didn't back up. "I don't have anything to do with your dad dying. He has cancer. He is going to die and the doctors can't help him."

"You're a liar. Mom said you would say that. You're killing dad, and one day I will kill you."

The grandmother responded, "Do you want to see your dad? He is in the room right there." She gestured toward it.

Piper shouted, "You stay away from us, you hear? Betty will go in with us and you are not allowed to come in."

The African American woman stepped forward and introduced herself as Mrs. Stone's personal assistant, Betty. Later, I overheard Elle Hawk tell one of the visitors that Betty originally came to work for the Stones after Piper was born. She was hired to feed Piper at night because Mrs Stone took Ambien and couldn't wake up to feed baby. Betty stayed on as a sitter, and then again as a night feeder to Milo. Now Betty had assumed the role as personal assistant.

Milo and Piper went into their dad's room with Betty, while the teenage babysitter waited out in the hall, Mrs. Stone came out of hiding and joined her children. Mitch Stone's niece was in the room with him, and the kids were glad to see her. It was OK with their mother for her to stay. While in the room, the niece heard Piper tell her mother, "Gran should be shot for killing Dad." I heard the niece report this to Elle Hawk.

When Mrs. Stone left the room with her children, her personal assistant approached Elle Hawk, "Carlotta asked me to deliver this message. She said that you and your daughters are not allowed to see or speak to Milo and Piper. If you approach the children in any way, she will get a restraining order."

Elle Hawk said, "You are a church-going woman. I know this not only by the gold cross you wear around your neck, but Mitch told me you sang in the choir, and he had to ask you to quit preaching to his kids about the Lord. What do you, as a Christian woman, think about a mother telling her children that their grandmother is murdering their father, and that their grandmother and aunts are not allowed to see them? How bad is that going to fuck up their tender minds, Betty? And why are you, as a Christian, going along with it?"

Betty puffed up and informed Elle Hawk, "I pray for this family every day. I ask the Lord to watch over those children and I have done so since they came into this world. That's what I do for them. I pray."

It was a heavy scene—the little, gray-haired white woman in a face-up with the big black woman. I'd say at least ten visitors heard that exchange, and it stunned them into silence.

It was on the fifth day, the first wife told Elle Hawk that the current wife had removed the patient's Fentanyl patches. I figured Mrs. Stone was applying them to her own body. That was not an uncommon thing to do. We could have reported her for stealing narcotics but didn't.

We keep the booklet "*Gone From My Sight: The Dying Experience*" at the nurses station, and I gave a copy to Mrs. Stone on day one. She dropped it at my feet and said in a real quiet voice, almost like a hiss, "I'm not going to read that negative shit." The look on her face, placid, the sound of her voice, soft, didn't match the hostility of her words. Elle Hawk had read the copy I gave her, and she understood what her son needed to die—peace.

Hawk told me that her sister's son had died the

same way as Mitch. In fact, he was in this same hospice, and she asked if I remembered Max Walker. I certainly did. I knew Mrs. Stone reminded me of someone, and now I remembered who—she was a lot like Mrs Walker—small, spoiled, mean, and a trouble maker. As I recall, Walker's mother also had her son's health care proxy.

I waited for Mitch's Stone's sister to leave the room so I could fill out the paperwork as soon as he passed away. His mother was not there. She told me the evening before that she expected her son to die within the next twenty-four hours and didn't want to see it. She said holding her grandmother's hand when she died, sitting next to her husband on the beach while he died, holding her pet parrot of nineteen years while he died, was enough close-up dying for her.

Later, I heard, at almost the same minute her plane was landing in Maui, her son was taking his last breath. Hearing that gave me what Hawaiians call "da chicken skin." I had the same feeling when I came on duty and learned there had been no visitors all day except his big sister. I wondered if there was something in the air that warned the others away.

Only certain kinds of nurses and doctors can work in the electrified air where the unexplainable happens Being near the dying makes me feel alive or remember to actively live.

The door finally opened and his sister stepped

out of the room looking like she was about to drop. Mrs. Stone got in her face and spoke real slow and soft. "Do not come to the funeral. You are not invited. Now, get out. He is all mine now."

Mitch Stone's sister didn't move. She stood in front of the door for a few seconds. I guess she was collecting her thoughts. I was thinking, *hurry up, I need to get in there and write up my report.*

She finally spoke, "All that's left in that room is a husk—it's all yours, Carlotta."

Mitch Stone's sister thanked me for helping her brother and went to each member of the staff on the floor and did the same.

CHAPTER 9 — CARLOTTA STONE

A month after Mitch died, I met with attorney Peter Parsons. He's a member of the oldest and most prestigious firm in Arkansas. Hillary worked there when Bill was Governor. I liked that. I wanted a strategy to break Mitch's plan to ruin my life.I needed a smart guy. My sister said Parsons is supposed to be the best negotiator in the state. I like winners.

Lee Edwards did a background on Parsons. He called to let me know he'd completed his report and I asked him to give me the highlights and email the rest.

"Parsons is thirty-six, his wife Sylvia, a year older, a stay at home mom, his only child is a boy, nine. They've a heavy mortgage and live two block from Little Rock Country Club, a few doors down from her parents, tons of debt, and he supports his widowed mother. Parsons didn't come from money, but his wife does. Her father is an executive at Stephens, Inc. and her mother came from a prominent Little Rock family."

"Are they members of the Country Club? My mom has been a member for years and Mitch and I are too. I love the club and it's history. I'm going to keep our membership. The kids will need the club experience, don't you think."

I guess Lee was looking through the info because he didn't answer right away. "The Parsons and her parents are members. The wife was a debutante, cheerleader at U of A, worked as a preschool teacher before she married Parsons. Her brother is an attorney, works for Walmart, he introduced them."

"Are they close? I mean, did he marry her for her contacts or are they a tight couple?"

"Hard to say. For a busy attorney, he spends a lot of time with his kid. Goes to his ball games, to the after-school practice, stays maybe an hour, enough to count. Drops him off to school every morning."

I wanted Lee to know that I had done some investigation myself. "I read about Peter on the Rosenberg website. On the *Meet Our Attorneys* page, it said most of his practice was in tax law for corporations, and he also did things for banks that managed trusts. I guess that's why he'll be good for me. I like his looks. In his pictures, he wears a bow tie and suits that don't fit tight, kind of like what someone my dad's age would wear."

Edwards continued, "Parsons and WP Kelpe both graduated with honors from Hendrix College with masters in accounting, both attended Bowen Law School. Parsons is a negotiator, not a litigator."

I didn't know what he meant by him being a negotiator not a litigator but I figured it wasn't important. "I can't wait to meet him. We have an appointment at the end of the week. I'm trying to decide what to wear. I need to look just right. What does his wife look like?"

Lee described her as "very tall, slim but muscular, shoulder length brown hair with blond highlights She spends a lot of time in yoga classes, rowing, spinning. She lifts weights and dresses to show off her athletic body. An attractive woman but not pretty."

"Do you have a list of her friends?"

Edwards gave me the names of three women Sylvia Parsons went to grade school with and had remained friends with over the years. Aside from them, the other women he saw with her were in her yoga classes. He gave me those names too. "She went with a group of women this past year for yoga retreats in Bali and another trip to Sedona. I haven't found a boyfriend if that's what you are asking. She has lunch with Parsons on Wednesdays at the Copper Kettle."

I asked Lee what he thought—were they happy together? "Give me your gut feeling."

"My gut tells me that you will figure out what you need to know when you get to know him better. I deal in facts; that's why you hired me. I'm not psychic." He gave a little laugh when he said it. "I just sent the complete report to your email. Call if you have questions."

When I got to Peter Parsons' office for our first meeting, the receptionist told me to take a seat and asked what I'd like to drink and brought me a Diet Coke, but no straw. Peter walked out into the reception area and greeted me. He gave me his condolence speech. It sounded like a script, but then he put his hand on my shoulder and we walked into his office.

Peter was probably a foot and a little more taller than me. Mitch was on the short side of medium, but with more muscle than Parsons had on him. Anyway, Peter directed me to a comfortable chair and went around and sat down at his desk. I laid my cell on his desk, but I didn't tell him I was recording our meeting.

I looked the part of the widow in need of a man to save me. I figured that was the way to go. Play helpless. I wore a simple beige Oscar de La Renta dress, set off with a double strand of black Tahitian pearls around my throat and earrings to match. I thought Peter looked at me like he cared, and he would save me from being taken advantage of by a greedy lawyer. I put on my wounded-woman-in-need mask and said things like, "I can't tell you how much I appreciate this meeting. I'm starting to feel better already."

Peter listened as I told him why I needed his help. I know I spent a lot of that time obsessing over WP and Elle Hawk, as trust protector, but he needed to know how evil those two are. I told him how WP had taken complete control over my life and I was terribly afraid of him. Sometimes, I had to dab at my eyes. I guess he thought it was sadness, but my new woven eyelashes were a little long and were irritating my eyes

“WP has inserted himself into every area of my life. When I need something extra he asks all sorts of questions. He even came out to my house with an inspector and said he needed to document its condition. He said that was in the trust rules. I don’t believe that.He was spying on me. He’s a stalker.”

I didn’t tell him WP was a Boy Scout leader and all those guys were perverts, like priests. I wanted to say it, but I knew it would be over the top, and besides, Peter might be Catholic or a Scout leader. I guess I got my point across because he said he understood my feelings of powerlessness and fear. At first, Peter didn’t notice my cell phone sitting on his desk. Then he picked it up and saw I was recording us. But he didn’t say anything, just set it back down. I think that meant he accepts me as I am.

After an hour, he got real official sounding. “Carlotta, I need to get ready for another appointment. I usually don’t represent clients outside of the corporate world. Your legal issues are very complex and disturbing, and I would like to help you. But first, I need to study the documents, meet with you again, and then we can determine whether I’m the right attorney for your case.”

I didn’t respond at first. His words surprised me. “I know you *are* perfect for me. I can just tell it, and I feel it. Trust me, I have good instincts about that sort of thing." I stood up and walked over to his desk. I looked at him and said in a shaky, soft voice, "Spending time thinking about representing me isn't going to work for me, Peter. I'm scared and I need your help."

Peter pulled himself up out of his chair and stood next to his desk. I guess he didn't want me standing over him. "I totally understand how vulnerable you feel. How hard it is to trust. But to be fair with you, I need time to study the case and give you my analysis of what we can and cannot accomplish. I don't want to disappoint you."

"I don't want to be disappointed either but," I stopped for emphasis and said as sweetly as I could, "take my case today or I'll find a man who isn't afraid of a challenge." I opened my handbag, took out a check for fifty-thousand dollars, and laid it on the desk.

He hesitated, but I knew he needed the money. Still, he didn't pick it up. Instead, he said, "If you're sure, I'll have my assistant bring in our client agreement and you can take it home and look it over." I knew I had him when he said that. Then he pissed me off. "Maybe you should run this by JoAnne. I want you to be sure."

"My big sister doesn't make my decisions. Either we make a deal today or not at all." Again, I kept t soft, but I was seething inside.

Peter asked his assistant to come in. I signed the agreement without reading it. He was my man now. He didn't mention that the retainer was ten thousand dollars and I had handed him fifty. The check was my way to let him know I was willing to spend a lot of money to win over Mitch's trust protector and his lawyer.

Then he said, "Carlotta, now that we're going to work together, I need to know everyone you've spoken with about your concerns with the way WP Kelpe has handled your situation, your problems with your mother-in-law, and a list of everyone who has helped you so far." I thought, *holy shit* "Why? That sounds like a lot of work"

"It helps me to have a complete background. If you like, my paralegal can meet with you and the two of you can work on that. It really will be helpful."

"Okay, If that's what you need."

Two weeks later, Peter got my mountain of information. It took his legal assistant around twenty-five hours to assemble what I had. It included transcriptions of all the secret recordings of phone and in-person conversations I'd had with WP Kelpe and others at his firm; footage of Mitch's various sickrooms and the conversations that took place there; the fight over missing pain medication and Elle Hawk ripping the sheet off the sleeping nurse; a text sent to me by her five hours after Mitch died and a whole lot more.

Peter called and said he wanted to meet and go over some things. I went to his office after I dropped the kids off at school. It was a little early for me to get dressed up and have a business meeting. I usually take the kids while I'm still in my pajamas but winning this war was my mission. When I got to his office, his para-legal took me to the conference room where Peter was waiting. Everything I'd sent over was laid out on the long table. She stayed for the meeting. I didn't like that.

Peter got right down to business. "I am shocked at the text Mitch's mother sent you just hours after he died. I had the screenshot blown up to fit a sheet of regular paper. I can see this as an example of her hostility toward you." He read it out loud as if I had forgotten the curse.

You have the husk, but we had the man. You are cruel to have taken a dying man's comfort from him. He suffered a week when the judge granted the TRO based on your lies. I hope you suffer as he did at the hands of the children, who I hope will see you as the selfish person you are. It is fitting that you were absent when he died. He did not want you there. So go have your empty future. You have no idea what he planned for you.

He put the paper down."I felt a little chill cross over me when I read this the first time. It reminded me of the scene in Stephen King's novel,*Thinner*, when the old gypsy pointed and said, 'thinner' and the guy he cursed rapidly started losing weight."

I had no clue what he was talking about, but I

acted like I did and then I said, "I thought that text was a curse."

"The text isn't enough to prove she can't be objective and should be removed as trust protector, but it is a start." Peter asked what she meant about 'taking a dying man's comfort' and about the TRO. I told him she accused me of taking Mitch's pain patches and said I had lied in court about Mitch talking.

I felt that his question was a challenge. "Don't you forget, she is a great liar and the things she wrote about me were lies." I think he got what I was saying—watch out for the trust protector.

"I am astounded by the number of people you have consulted and the time they have spent answering your questions on the trust, but . . ."I interrupted. "I was conducting research and building a case to break that evil trust. I could have been a lawyer like my sister, but she's not rich like I am because I married a wood chopper."

He hesitated, "I am not sure what you mean by a wood chopper but it isn't good that so many people in town know this much about your problems with the trust and that you want to break it. We need to reshape the issue into—I am not contesting the trust; I am questioning Kelpe's competency as trustee. Our case will be about conflict of interest and other legal issues concerning Kelpe. It is not a contest to the Stone Trust."

"I don't get what you mean. It is about breaking the trust. I thought you understood that." I sat back down next to him not across the table and told his assistant to go get me a Diet Coke but she called the receptionist to bring it, I felt like they were ganging up on me.

"We cannot approach it from that direction. The trust has a no-contest clause and the courts in Arkansas usually uphold those, and we don't want to go to court. We want to negotiate not litigate."

"Negotiation not litigation?"

"Yes, yes, I see you get it."

Actually, I was trying to remember where I'd heard those two words used together before.

"I'm glad we are on the same page. What you need to do now is to keep quiet and not discuss this case with anyone but me. I am impressed you had Mitch's computers and emails hacked by Guardian Forensics to capture and preserve the data. How did you know about that company?"

"One of the people I'd been talking to told me. See, it was a good thing I asked so many people to help me—this is a good example."

Peter said many of the documents contained privileged attorney-client communications between Kelpe and Mitch regarding the trust and his company's business. "It worries me that you gave these documents to a variety of people such as the accountant who works for your mother; your husband's insurance agent; your sister; a lawyer friend of yours who has a child in the same school as your children; a retired trust lawyer who is a friend of your sister; a lawyer that is your neighbor; Is there anyone else?"

"Well, let me think. Jim Worth's been working on taking down Kelpe and the trust protector on the personal level. He told me to make friends with WP's wife and undermine their marriage. My investigator said Kelpe's wife had a prescription drug problem in the past. She went to rehab once or twice. He said she's well now and volunteers at her kid's school."

I wasn't sure if I should, but I went on. "Jim said it would be easy to push her over the edge. I could let it slip to her that WP was fooling around on her, anything that would cause her to pick up the pill bottle or file for divorce. That would distract Kelpe. And, she has a seriously ill father who probably won't live out the year, and she gets a big inheritance free of a trust. Worth said If she thinks WP is stealing from a client like me, she would believe he would figure out a clever way to steal her inheritance. She would want a divorce before her father died. I've already had coffee with her a couple of times. Worth's going to set Hawk up to make her look like she is a little bit crazy and not objective so she can't be trust protector. He's good at things like that and then . . . "

"Carlotta, stop right there. I don't want to know anything about that. I play by the rules and I win by using them."

That threw me a little. "I wouldn't really do any of those things. I just wanted you to know what Worth thought." I didn't like Peter's stuffy approach to problem solving. At that moment, I wondered if he was the right man for me, but the Rosenberg firm was so famous and well respected, I let it go.

There is a lot of hate coming off me. I know that, I embrace it, but I thought I had hidden it from Peter. I hated Mitch for dying and taking away my big spending ways; I hated him for controlling me from the grave; I hated his mother, his sisters; my stepchildren, his attorney; the doctors who said he didn't have a chance to live; the judge who agreed that his mother had the legal right to make medicals decisions for him. Who else was on my list? Well, Peter would be if he didn't win lots of money for me free of Mitch's control.

"I know you think I'm obsessed with the trust protector. See, I told you, I can't even say her name. JoAnne said that twenty percent of my recorded conversations with Kelpe contained rants about *her* and that makes me look bad. Like when I said to Kelpe, 'What if the trust protector just happened to have an accident and die?' and then he told me not to say things like that. On another tape, I was going on about her and asked him, 'Have you ever heard of the Dixie Mafia?' and WP said, 'Only on *Justified,* and then he told to quit talking about her."

Peter looked at his assistant and then back at me. "I need to know. Would you hire someone to harm Elle Hawk?"

"Never! Sometimes when I am tired and worried, I binge-watch too much television and get a little dramatic. I was just acting out when I said those things. My life has been so stressful since Mitch passed."

"Well, I don't want to become a Bill MacArthur." He stood up and I got the message—our meeting was over.

I didn't know who he was talking about. After I left his office, I looked up the name. He was a Little Rock lawyer, and his client, Mary Lee Orsini, had had MacArthur's wife murdered, and it ruined MacArthur's career. I didn't understand what that had to do with me.

The next time we met, Peter had outlined a plan. He wasn't ready to put it down on paper yet and wanted to hear what I thought. Like the last visit, we didn't go to his office but to the conference room and the same assistant was in there and she stayed. He pulled out a chair and I took a seat. Instead of sitting at the end of the table so we would be side-sitting, he went around the table and sat across from me.I wondered what that was all about.

"Basically, I will do the thinking and planning and hire other attorneys to file the lawsuits we might need if Kelpe won't agree to negotiate, but I am confident that he will. I'll go over the steps. First, we will create a conflict of interest. It will take a team of attorneys from other firms and help from accountants to set up Kelpe and create this conflict. We will claim Kelpe was representing you and Mitch at the same time. I want you to schedule regular meetings with Kelpe and ask for personal and legal advice, reinforcing you want to work with him as a team, ask him to do legal work for you. And you keep on recording it all."

I made a little laugh. "I thought you didn't use tactics like secret recordings. What about *I only play by the rules* speech you gave me."

"Carlotta, I was talking about deliberately destroying someone personal life not recording conversations. Let's move on. In step two, I will research and recommend the firm you will hire to challenge Kelpe as executor of Mitch's will. The point here is to see how he responds."

"I thought the trust is what's important, so what does a will have to do with anything?" I felt my index finger go to my hair to twist it around as is my habit and put my hands in my lap. I saw on some talk show the other day that this is a self-comforting habit.

“I will explain that later. Let’s get on with the plan. In step three, Jim Worth will file on behalf of your children a lawsuit against Elle Hawk as trustee of the Beck Trust. That will create a conflict of interest with her. I can see I need to explain. When Mitch died, his interest in the Beck Trust went to his kids. Worth will question Hawk’s actions as trustee just like the Beck girls are doing.”

“But they keep losing to her. Why would we do that?”

“The point is, we want to create conflict of interest.”

”I don’t get it but go on.”

“In step four, you put a request before the trust protector to see if she decides for or against you. Worth will take care of that too. And in step five, I hire a firm that specializes in malpractice to file a complaint against Kelpe, if he won’t negotiate a settlement. The threat of a malpractice will soften him up and he will negotiate and hand over twenty-five million dollars free of trust. In exchange, you take yourself out of the trust, and the malpractice against Kelpe goes away.”

“That’s a lot of plan. It sounds like it will take a long time. It's so complicated. There’s got to be quicker way for me to get my money?”

“We can't take this head on and directly challenge Kelpe as trustee. That will invoke the no-contest clause and that means litigation. I prefer negotiation and this plan will bring Kelpe to the table." He laughed and said, "Hell, I don't even know where the courthouse is located."

Then he threw me a curveball. "This is going to get expensive in attorney fees. We're going to hire several firms to make this plan work. You might want to consider a contingency agreement over the fee-based we have. If we decide on contingency, I will get one-third of the settlement but I don't charge your for my time if we lose. In our current arrangement, win or lose, you pay me. Think about it."

After I left the meeting, I called my sister. As usual, it took a long time for her to call back. I sat in my car and went to a legal website so I could better understand about the contingency thing. It was complicated so I drove home. About an hour later she called me back and I asked her what she would do about the contingency. She asked a bunch questions about our meeting before answering me.

"From what you told me, Peter sounds confident he can negotiate a settlement, but I don't think Kelpe will go for it. Are you going to be happy giving him a little over eight million if he gets the twenty-five? I don't think legal fees will cost close to that."

"He didn't explain it exactly like that. What would you do?"

She didn't answer that but asked me, "Did Peter tell you what would happen if Kelpe claims you are challenging the trust and violating the no-contest clause?"

"He said we were not contesting the trust. His plan is to put pressure on Kelpe to negotiate a settlement."

"Do you want to know what could happen if he is wrong and Kelpe does what I just said?"

I wanted to know and said so.

"Your monthly income from the trust will stop until the matter is decided by a judge, and that might take a year, maybe longer. You would have to use what you have in the bank to live on. How much available cash and other securities do you have? What do you have in your checking account? How much is your cost of living for one year?"

"I don't know any of that. Kelpe's office handles all of it for me."

"You're telling me you don't know how much money you have to live on if WP suspends your allowance and quits paying the bills. That is shocking, Carlotta. I thought you were smarter than that."

“Before Mitch died, his accountant paid all the household the bills. Now, WP’s office takes care of it for me. I never have to think about those things .”

“Carlotta, I’ve got to go. You need to think hard about going down this dangerous road Peter’s got you on. Bird in the hand—that’s what I think.”

CHAPTER 10 — ELLE HAWK

Almost six months had passed since Mitch died and the way he died still haunted me. I couldn't listen to country music and drink beer at the same time without crying. I was on my way down to the North Shore for my morning swim, listening to a book on tape while driving the curvy back road from upcountry.

It was a road that claimed a half-dozen lives a year because it was narrow, had limited sight distance, and wove through sugarcane fields. It was my favorite road because not many tourists knew about it. Harvey wouldn't drive it at night—that was when most of the accidents occurred—but I did. Death didn't mean much to me. I just hoped when it came, it was quick, like it was for Harvey and my father and grandfathers; fast, no time to think.

My cell rang and I answered the call from Clarence Doyle's office. It was his paralegal. We had become friends over the years.

"I have gossip. I heard Carlotta was seen at the Rosenberg Firm having a meeting with Peter Parsons. It was last week. My guess is, she's hired him to get rid of you and WP and set the stage to get free."

I pulled off on a narrow patch before the spot where cell coverage usually failed. It was then I noticed the white Toyota pass by and then turn around to go back in the opposite direction. It was a local car, not a lost tourist.

I was looking in the rearview mirror while

listening. I interrupted, “Something’s wrong. This car passed me and came back, and now it’s pulled in front of me and stopped. Oh no! A really big guy is getting out and coming toward me. Stay on the line.”

I touched the lever to put the car in drive but there wasn’t time for me to move it before the brute, at least six foot two and close to three hundred pounds, was pressing himself against the driver’s side door. He tried the handle. The door was locked. I couldn’t see his face, just his Hawaiian print shirt and Lone Star belt buckle.

He leaned around and put his baboon face next to the windshield, showed his nicotine-stained teeth in a grin, and mouthed, *You are served*. He shoved the papers under the wiper blade, turned and walked toward the waiting Toyota. The driver was standing next to it with a cell phone held high in her hand.

“Stay on the line. It’s a process server.”

I jumped out of my car, grabbed the papers, and ran after him, yelling, “What’s your name?” He kept walking. I reached him and slapped him on the back of the neck with the rolled-up papers. “Turn around, you coward.”

The server kept walking, opened the door of the passenger side, and sat down. Before he could shut the door, I put my 105-pound body between it and the big man. “I asked you your name.”

Very slowly, he said, “I don’t have to answer your

questions. You steal from your grandchildren. My name is Tony Mirada and you're a thief. People like you make me sick."

The driver of the car, a small, dark-haired local woman still had her phone in her hand, recording the event. She began shouting, "Don't be mad at us. We're just the messengers. We're just the messengers."

I ignored her. "Tony, you're a process server, not a judge. It isn't your job to interpret the paperwork and decide my innocence or guilt." I tapped him on the front of his chest with the rolled-up papers. "Got it?" I stepped away from their car and walked back to mine.

"You won't believe what just happened." I told myself to breathe. My body vibrated with excitement. I gave her a blow-by-blow. "Give me a second to look at this." I glanced through the summons. "Worth is her attorney, not Parsons. He represents Carlotta for Milo and Piper—it's a lawsuit against me as Beck trustee, same kind of thing as the Beck Sisters. I guess the game is on, round one, to get me removed as trust protector. That didn't take long. I guess she's finished mourning."

"Elle! That was dangerous, to have gone after the server and hit him. It will look bad. They're going to try to profile you as a nut."

"What? A little, gray-haired woman in a muumuu running down a brute and slapping the back of his thick neck with a rolled-up paper?
The whole thing was so exciting, it made my day, and

it's only nine in the morning Hawaii time. That doesn't sound a bit crazy to me."

I called my neighbor who worked for the police department and asked about the process servers. I learned both had been cops. They'd retired a couple of years ago and started a PI business.

Doyle called me the next day and confirmed what I thought. "Elle, this is the beginning of an attempt to create a conflict of interest between you and the beneficiaries. Worth filed a petition called a designation of master or receiver in circuit court against you as the Beck trustee. It alleges you've breached your fiduciary duty as trustee to the detriment of Piper and Milo,"

He went on to say that both of the process servers had sent letters to Worth regarding their service to me, and Worth had already filed it with the court as an exhibit. They claimed they had tried to serve me for over a week but I'd purposely avoided them.

I pulled up the Pulaski County Court site while we talked. "Doyle, this duo has been watching the wrong house and following the wrong car. My car was described as blue. It's gray. My house was described as having motion detectors in the yard; it doesn't, but the house next door does, and the owner drives a blue Subaru—fools."

"Don't go beating up on any more process servers. Anyway, Carlotta can't proceed with this lawsuit.

First, she has to be appointed guardian of the children's estate by the court. Worth should have known that."

"Why does the court have to appoint her guardian of her own children's estate?" Doyle explained how the legalities of all that worked. A week later, Worth corrected his mistake but the judge didn't make Carlotta guardian because I intervened in the case. The judge appointed a lawyer to do the guardian job. Round one to me and Mitch.

CHAPTER 11 — CARLOTTA STONE

I couldn't believe it when the judge didn't make me guardian of finances for my own children. I didn't know that a mother had to have permission from a court to take care of her children's money.

I blame Worth for that. When he filed that thing against Mitch's mother and didn't do it right, that got her attention. If he hadn't fucked it up in the first place, she wouldn't have known I filed for guardian of their finances. Having Worth file it was Parsons' idea and his mistake, and I won't forget it. Maybe Worth is getting old or sick. He's lost a lot of weight and had an operation for something to do with a stent, whatever that is.

Now I have another man ruling my life. I don't like the attorney that was appointed. I think that judge has something against me anyway. He's the one who upheld the health care proxy and I lost that one too.

The guardian is a pompous asshole and a coward. He won't even meet with me without his paralegal present. He doesn't answer my calls but returns them with someone on the line with him—calls it a conference call. I would have liked to have slapped him in the face when he told me, "I don't work for you, Mrs. Stone. I work for your children and their financial well-being. I've explained that before and, as I recall, so did the judge."

I called Peter and let him how the guardian treated me. My words weren't soft and neither were my questions. I asked him why he got Worth to take on that part of the plan, and Peter said Worth had a lot of experience with trusts and he was surprised with the mistake. I said, "Well, in the beginning you said we would use experts in each field. So why didn't you pick one for this?" I was gently letting him know he'd fucked up without saying it.

Peter ignored the question. "Carlotta, it doesn't matter Hawk intervened and the court appointed a guardian. It shows she is hostile to you and that is what we want. We need evidence she is not objective. This is good."

"I hadn't thought of it that way." I kidded him. "You really know how to spin, and I suppose that is a good trait, because I'm good at that myself. All of this is so complicated, there are so many things I still don't get."

"I'm going to explain as clearly as I can, so be patient." I was recording it because the first time he told me, my phone ran out of juice.

"The important thing to remember is we are creating a documented conflict of interest. We aren't finished with the trust protector yet. Remember, you were supposed to get two million if Mitch still held an active pilot's license. Kelpe refused to give it to you free and clear and put the two million in another trust that benefits the family as a whole. We're going take Kelpe's decision in front of the trust protector. Remember, if a beneficiary disagrees with the trustee, the trust protector decides."

“If it’s up to her, she won’t give me a thing, so why bother?” I wondered if all this was just a way for him to increase his billing hours.

“As I’ve explained before, If she decides against you, we can use it to show she isn’t objective when it comes to you. Putting the active pilot’s license question before her is another move toward eradicating her.” Peter should have left it at that, but then he said, “It’s not a big deal, you still get some benefit from the two million and more proof she is not objective—we want that.”

I couldn’t help it; I raised my voice maybe a little too much, “That money is mine, all mine, and no one should get a penny of it except me. You’re supposed to be a good negotiator, so negotiate and get me all of my money.”

I think I upset him. He brushed me off, said he had another call he had to take and would get back with me. “Carlotta, I think it would be beneficial for you to see a grief counselor.”

“What does that mean? That sounds like a pot shot. Are you calling me crazy and need a shrink.”

“I didn’t mean it like that. You’ve mentioned several times how stressful you life has become. You are grieving the loss of your husband and grief produces stress. A counselor who specializes in this will help you adjust to the terrific blow you and you children received when Mitch died. I am so sorry if I upset you. I was trying to help."

"Maybe you're right about a person to help me with grief. I'll check around on that." I didn't mean a word of it, but I didn't want to alienate him. I didn't believe he was sorry; he was covering his ass. That's why we meet in the conference room and his assistant stays the whole time. I intimidate him. I liked him better when we met alone in his office.

A couple of days later his assistant called and asked if I had time to speak with Peter. I said I would if he called back in an hour. I could have talked then, but I wanted him to wait and I'm glad I did. He heaped more stress my way with his news.

When I answered Peter's call he started off hot, no warm up, "The trust protector got the request for a decision on the airplane matter, and she turned it over to Clarence Doyle. He contacted lawyers from the FAA and was told Mitch wasn't an active pilot because he didn't have a health certificate. You don't get the two million outright."

"You are telling me the bottom line is, Elle Hawk has won another round over us. Is that right?" I was glad I was lying down under my tree when this call came. I knew exactly where I was going to string him up.

Peter didn't answer so I said, "I'm going to get even with that trust protector in my own way because you can't handle her."

"Carlotta, it would be a good idea to keep those thoughts to yourself."

I knew I was exposing myself and that I wasn't hiding anything by using a soft voice instead of screaming at him like I wanted to. My life was flying out of control. I called Worth. He's more my kind of man than Mr. Smarty Pants Parsons. We think more alike when it comes to a certain kind of thinking.I filled Worth in on Parsons' defeats and he devised a plan that would bring Elle Hawk back to Little Rock. It sounded confusing when he explained it.

"It's time for depositions and mediation in the Beck sister's case against Hawk as trustee for Beck Trust. I'll contact Doyle and schedule these things, that will bring her into our territory."

"Does that mean you are going set a trap and we are going to catch a rat?"

Worth laughed and didn't answer.

CHAPTER 12 — ELLE HAWK

I didn't get back to Little Rock until a year after Mitch died. I wouldn't have gone then if I hadn't had to deal with the Beck sisters' lawsuits against me. Jim Worth wanted to do depositions and mediation in the case.

I planned to arrive the day before the deposition and leave the day after the mediation. I'd written and called Peter Parsons and asked to see Piper and Milo. He didn't turn me down in writing or by phone call, or by contacting Doyle; he just ignored me. I took my usual American flight that arrived in Little Rock mid morning.

When I landed in Dallas that morning, a text message popped up on my phone from Doyle: "Call me as soon as you land at DFW. Urgent!" I called and he said, "Elle, listen and don't ask questions. I'll explain later. I'm on a call on the other line. I was told you'd be followed by someone Carlotta hired when you get here. I've rented you a car at DFW. Do not fly in. Call me when you drop the car off in North Little Rock and I'll pick you up. I'm texting you the car info now." He hung up before I could ask him any questions.

I called Lee Edwards two hours outside Texarkana. He said he didn't know what Golden Eyelash Viper was up to. She was holding her cards close, which was unusual for her. No one knew about our relationship. I'd not even told Birdie about Lee's promise to Mitch or the half million that had appeared in his account the morning after he saw Mitch in the hospital.

Doyle met me at the rental drop-off and we drove to the Marriott in downtown Little Rock. We went to the room he'd reserved and he drank a Martini to relax and I had a double shot of Don Julio and a beer.

Doyle took his time getting around to telling me what was going on. "I got a call from a private investigator I trust. He said he'd heard Carlotta Stone had met several times with an individual in the *personal retribution business*, and you were the target."

"Who's the investigator?" I wondered if it was Lee Edwards but didn't want to say that name.

"I don't think you know James Thomas."

He was right, I didn't know the name. "Do you seriously think Carlotta has plans to have someone cripple or kill me?"

"Guys in that kind of business don't usually murder anyone; maiming is good enough. And don't forget about those two brutes the hospice nurses thought were trying to kidnap Mitch. That was strange. You can laugh, I get that, but I say let's play it safe."

"Are you kidding? I feel like we are characters in one of those binge-watching-on-a-rainy-day shows that Carlotta's addicted to."

"Elle, not long ago an accountant was running on the back trails over at the Big Dam Bridge and a jogger found him beaten to a pulp. He has a glass eye now. Then there was the plastic surgeon who was robbed in his home and his fingers and hands were crushed. His career as a surgeon is over."

"Wow. I guess I need an on-line subscription to *Arkansas Democrat-Gazette* to keep up with the drama in Little Rock."

"Just a couple of weeks ago, a woman finished her workout at the Athletic Club and found her front tire flat. While she was calling AAA, someone broke her ankles. She won't run the Boston Marathon again next year, or ever."

I said, "Oh, I remember now. Mitch told me his maid's teenage daughter was found in his quarry. Turtles had eaten part of her face by the time she was found; she was dead. That got to Mitch. He started keeping more guns around and bumped up his home security."

"I want you to stay in your room. Quarantine yourself. Tomorrow, I'll come and we'll go to the deposition together. I'll know if we're being followed when we leave Worth's office."

"If Carlotta is so determined to hurt me, she doesn't have to wait until I'm in Little Rock. She knows where I live. Remember, that process server I slapped. He was working for Worth."

"Don't go to the hotel restaurant or even think about going for a walk along the river or around town. I'll be back in the morning."

The next day, Doyle picked me up around eight and we went to The Root restaurant for breakfast and then Worth's office for the deposition. His firm was on the tenth floor, with a view of the Arkansas River from the north-facing wall of windows and the parking lot on the South side. When we entered the conference room, the Beck sister and Worth were sitting at the long table. She had Worth's suit jacket draped over her shoulders. I wondered what that was about, and then I remembered they had gone to high school together.

Worth introduced himself to me and indicated that I should sit at the head of the table. He made no attempt at small talk. One of his junior partners sat next to the Beck sister, and the videographer stood at the end of the table facing me, with his camera on a tripod. Doyle sat across from Worth, and the court reporter was present and seated.

I hadn't met Worth before, but I was shocked to see a man looking like he belonged in a hospital bed. His suit pants were cinched tight around his waist, showing he'd lost about five inches from his middle. I wondered why he didn't buy new pants or have these altered. His face, nearly skeletal, was a cruel one, from his sneering lips to his bushy brows hanging over his beady brown eyes. He kept a small red stress ball in his left hand and squeezed it off and on.

I got up and said I needed the ladies room before we started. Doyle followed me out the door. "Elle, you know how this goes. Be polite and . . ." I interrupted him.

"I know the drill. But I want to look out at the parking lot at your car to see if anyone is around it. I know it's a long shot, but who knows."

"I have someone down there already. Now, go get your game face on so we can get out of here sooner rather than later. I have a feeling this is going to be a marathon."

Doyle was right. Worth questioned me for six hours, with a short break for lunch. Then Doyle questioned the Beck sister for nearly two hours. I noticed Worth had a lot of stamina for a man looking so sick, but when it was over, when he could let down, and as we were leaving, I saw him go paler than he already was and stagger just a little before sitting back down.

As we took the elevator down, I said, "I bet that Jim Worth will be dead in six weeks."

"Well, I heard he just had a stent put in about six weeks ago."

"He's got something bad going on besides a stent. He looks like some of those guys who walked the halls at night in hospice pushing their IV poles along. He's a dead man walking. I can see that."

"I don't know. We're going to leave my car here and walk over to my office to talk about the mediation and what we will and won't negotiate."

I said again that I wouldn't give an inch, but I would play along because the court required it. I wanted to know why we weren't using his car and he said someone put a tracking device on it.

Late that afternoon, Doyle and I took a taxi from his office and went to a restaurant at the Capitol Hotel across the street from the Marriott. We could have walked, the hotel was close, but Doyle wasn't comfortable walking along the street with me. We'd come here so that his PI could see if we were followed and fifteen minutes into our dinner, he got a text we were.

I got up at six the next morning, showered and dressed in my outfit for the mediation: a pair of red denim slim-cut pants, a white, long-sleeved sweater, brown leather boots. I took the elevator down to the hotel coffee shop and bought a double espresso. I didn't think it would be a problem.

As I walked back across the lobby to the elevators, I noticed a woman sitting in a chair close to the entrance. I had spotted her there when I'd come down. Her posture was athletic and I could tell she was tall by the length of her legs. She wore her blond hair short and dressed like a person who worked at a bank, in a tight skirt, a jacket, and sensible shoes. She sat in a spot where she could see everyone coming in and going out. It looked like she was reading a newspaper while sipping a drink from Starbucks. I felt a little chill go through me, a premonition. She didn't fit. I turned around and walked back to the coffee shop and ordered a tall, hot mint tea and walked back toward the elevators.

I'd been stalked by process servers since

Harvey died, and I find myself scanning rooms before entering, constantly checking my rearview mirror, looking behind me to see if I'm being followed when I walk the beach. I am slightly hyper-vigilant and knew it could cause paranoia. Was I being paranoid?

I walked past the sitting woman again and as I did she got up and walked in the same direction. She didn't have a key card in her hand, and I noticed that because I had mine ready. The elevator wouldn't go past the third floor unless the room card was swiped. I imagined the woman would wait for me to get on first

I told myself that I'd been reading too many detective novels and it was feeding my paranoia. The elevator door opened and the woman waited. I made like I was going to get on, but I stumbled. My hot drink flew out of my hand and hit her skirt. She jumped.

"I'm sorry! I'm so clumsy. I hope that didn't burn you. I'll let someone know about the mess." But I didn't move. I was so nervous, I seemed to vibrate and freeze in place.

The woman shrugged and said, "No problem." She didn't act like it bothered her to have hot tea spilled all over her, and I thought that cool response was unnatural. I turned to go and about that time, a tall man dressed in a dark gray suit walked toward us. My heart beat fast as a hummingbird's wings. I felt pinned in by the two of them. The man stepped toward me and she stayed in place. When he pulled his jacket coat open, I nearly fainted. I saw his gun, and then a badge on his belt, and then my eyes focused on his unusual belt buckle.

"Bill Brass. LRPD."

Before I could say a word, my cell rang. It was Doyle and he wanted to speak to Brass. I handed him my cell. He listened and then told me that they were going to accompany me to Doyle's office and he'd explain what was happening when we got there. Brass introduced me to his partner and she went with me to my room so I could get my things, I wasn't coming back to the hotel. On the elevator, I peppered her with questions she politely refused to answer.

On the short ride, I spent my time thinking about what I knew of this detective. My sister Izzy met him when he worked a case about a kidnapped financial planner in Little Rock who lied to his local clients and caused them to lose their savings while he made his profit. He got away with it and someone wanted revenge. Brass focused his investigation on my sister's son, Max Walker, but couldn't prove his case. Mitch confided to me that Brass was right about Max and he'd given his cousin a small hand in what they called *The Halloween Prank*. The financial planner was found on Halloween night suspended in Delphi Pond with his head just above the water.He'd been there for several hours before a girl who lived in a house overlooking the pond discovered him. It was clear no one was trying to murder him, just teach him a lesson. When Max died, the case lost steam and went away.

Brass wrote a script about it and it became a limited series on Netflix. A year or two before that, he'd worked a case that inspired him to write a book. Brass became friends with my sister Izzy after Max died and that's how Mitch got to know him. He liked the detective. They used to go helicopter flying together and go out to Mitch's quarry and ride dirt bikes and practice shooting guns.

When I walked into Doyle's office the first thing he said was, "You were supposed to stay in your room. Why were you down in the lobby?"

"I wouldn't have had the adventure of meeting this famous detective if I'd obeyed." I looked at Brass and asked, "You still driving that 911 Carrera?"

"I sure am. Wouldn't be driving it now if Mitch hadn't teased me about the Boxster."

"He said you were proud of that car until he said it wasn't a real Porsche. When he raced you up the mountain and beat you with that souped of Cadillac sports car of his, you couldn't get rid of that Boxster fast enough. I heard all about that ride."

"Mitch had his way of letting a guy know when he needed to step of his game. You're wondering what's going on. Let have a talk." We walked into Doyle's small conference room and sat down alone and had a visit.

"I see you are still wearing that old belt buckle of Manny's. Mitch told me how attached to it you are. Lot of history in that hunk of silver."

Brass touched the buckle. “I’ll give you a quick summary of what we learned about the plans Carlotta made for your visit. You already know about the call made to Doyle by a local PI. The morning you were to arrive, Lee placed one of his female agents at the airport. She is about your size and was dressed in jeans wearing a red pack. When the flight you were supposed to be on landed, she walked out of the terminal, and picked up your rental car, spotted the car with two men in it following her, and notified Lee and he told his agent to drive toward West Little Rock and what roads to take. Lee called me, and a cop found a reason to pull that car over. The driver is in custody; his passenger jumped out of the car and fled. We found evidence that these men intended you harm. I can’t say more but we’re investigating.”

“That sounds like something straight out of a Scott Pratt novel. Are you on official police business or is this off the record work?”

“Sometimes it’s better to not say too much—just take care of the business at hand.”

There was a knock on the door before I had a chance to ask another question. Doyle said, “Elle we need to get going—mediation in thirty minutes.”

I stood and looked at Brass.”Thank you. Mitch said you would look out for me and the kids. I don’t want to go to mediation. I want more answers but I know you aren’t ready to give them.” I shook his hand and left with Doyle.

Mediation didn't last long. Worth wanted me to resign as Beck trustee, and give the Beck sister a million dollars, and then resign as trust protector for Mitch. I asked the mediator how Worth could demand I resign as trust protector when this case had nothing to do with Mitch's trust. She said it wasn't her job to explain anything. Her job was to deliver messages between the parties.

"Here is my message. I am not resigning anything or giving away any money. I am leaving right now. We are finished here." I felt my pointer finger go straight, and I badly wanted to shake it in the mediator's face, but I controlled myself. Mitch once said I should quit pointing at people when trying to make a point.

The mediator looked to Doyle, and he asked her to give us a moment. She left the room. I didn't wait for him to speak. I said, "I'm finished negotiating or mediating or whatever this five-hundred-dollar-an-hour bullshit is called. I'm out of here."

I left Little Rock without any answers. Kelpe hadn't contacted me as I had asked him to do. I wondered what was going on with him, why he was ignoring me. When the plane took off, I felt relieved to be leaving a place that represented so much drama. I wondered if I would ever come this way again.

CHAPTER 13 — WP KELPE

I sat at my desk and looked out at the Arkansas River, thinking about Mitch. It had been over a year since he died. It was his idea for me to buy this office building on the river, and that was a good call. I'd leased several of the office spaces, which paid a big part of the mortgage. Elle Hawk called a few days earlier to say she would be in Little Rock for matters in the Beck Trust lawsuit and wanted to see me, but I hadn't gotten back to her. Over the past year, my life had taken on a lot of complications and most of them came because of Carlotta Stone.

My personal life had in fact fallen apart. At first I thought it was because I was working over seventy hours a week trying to manage Carlotta and carry out Mitch's plans. Seventy was just my hours and didn't count the time other attorneys and accountants in my firm worked on the Stone matters too. Sure, my firm was getting paid for the work, but it was still a load. Carlotta and Mitch's adult daughters were exhausting, especially the younger one, Shelly. She was, as my mom liked to say, "Big talk on dry land."

JoAnne was constantly peppering me with questions. It took me hours to go through a thirty-five-page letter of single-spaced questions she said she "absolutely" needed to have answered for Carlotta who was calling and coming to the office all the time. She wanted me to draw up a codicil for her will and file paperwork for Mitch's social security, and so on, do things her sister could do for her. I complied because I wanted Carlotta to know she could count on me.

I felt obligated to get back with Elle because she was Mitch's mother, but I hadn't. I find her an edgy woman who makes me slightly uncomfortable most of the time. My firm started doing legal and accounting work for her after her husband died. Mitch had introduced us, but our business was conducted electronically or on the phone. I'd not met her in person until Mitch got sick.

I stretched out and put my feet up on my desk. I listened to my breath go in and out and relaxed. I'd learned the trick of dividing myself into two parts, a yin-yang, black-white sort of thing from Mitch, and was preparing to go there. It was a place where one part of my mind came up with an idea and the other hacked away at it and played the devil's advocate. Like Mitch, I found it useful.

Mitch and I had more than a few things in common including this devil's advocate approach to problem solving. Neither of us were big guys, or had fancy educations, or came from families with money or prestige. Both of us worked hard and didn't mind being underestimated because in the end we usually got what we wanted. We could out think and outwork most anyone else. To me, Mitch was my older brother from another mother.

I let my mind free flow and found myself remembering Mitch's first morning in hospice. On that morning over a year ago, I had gone to Mitch's room at around five in the morning. Elle was there, holding his hand, her phone playing country music, and she looked like she'd been there all night. I started to turn around and leave, but she saw me and got up.

"Glad you're here. I've been thinking we need to talk. There's a waiting room just outside the double doors. Let's go there. They have coffee and rolls. Mitch is resting, a nurse just put some new patches on him, and I don't want to stir him up. Dying is hard work."

I followed her out of the room, feeling uncomfortable that she wanted to have a talk, and the remark about dying being hard work. As my client, we got along well. She researched what she didn't understand before asking me questions that I often found challenging. Elle reminded me of Mitch that way. He looked a lot like her, and they had the same take-it-to-the-limit mentality.

Elle Hawk didn't ease into any subject that was on her mind. She was direct and to the point, and on this morning she was right on script. Before I could pour myself a cup of coffee, she started in on me.

"I don't think you've figured out that you're in for a lot of trouble as soon as Mitch dies. I see how you fluff up Carlotta, and I understand that. Problem is, she's already your enemy. Before you put up your shield of disbelief, listen to what I have to tell you."

She removed a smartphone from her backpack. "Remember the morning of the pee-pad-medication fight, the confrontation between me and JoAnne? I called you and you blew me off. Anyway, I took possession of JoAnne's phone for a short while and transferred what was on it to this." She handed me the phone.

"What you're going to learn is that a few days after Mitch was first hospitalized, Carlotta took his computer and his phone and had a company get all of Mitch's emails and texts regarding his estate planning, a copy of the trust documents, everything that she was never supposed to see, all of your emails to and from him regarding his company and personal business."

One thing about me is, I don't speak at times when people expect me to. I press my lips together and make an "umm" sound and tilt my head a little and wait. Silence can be a powerful tool, especially when I'm not sure what to say or how to react. I went into silent mode.

Elle waited and then went on talking. "Well, you get the picture. You'll learn she and her sister have hired a team of lawyers from at least three different law firms looking into the trusts and you for the purpose of having you removed as trustee. Carlotta will play nice, ask you for advice, ask you to do some legal work for her sister and so on. Her lawyer sister will ask you lots of questions, saying she's helping Carlotta to understand her financial future, but what she's really trying to do is create a conflict of interest and other problems for you." She handed me a hefty, manila envelope and said all I needed was in there.

"They also have plans to remove me as trust protector. And you'd better watch over your marriage. They'll come at you that way too. Now, I'm going. You go sit with Mitch and open my gift to you."

My head popped up off the back of the chair and I nearly fell off of it as my mind snapped back out of its reverie into the present. My feet hit the floor. Shit! Elle Hawk had given me that envelope over a year ago and I hadn't thought about it until this minute. I couldn't remember where I'd put it or if I'd thrown it away. I felt clammy and began searching through my filing cabinet, bookshelves, desk drawers.

I sat back down, went into a mindful state, and searched my memory banks. I saw myself go into Mitch's room. Elle was there, we talked, I put the envelope on a chair, my cell rang, I walked out of the room with the envelope. Still on the phone when I got to my car, I tossed the envelope into a box I kept in the trunk to store things I was going to look at later, non-urgent things. I got up from my desk and ran out to my car and found the envelope near the bottom of the pile. A year's worth of papers were stacked on top of it.

I rushed back to my office closed the door and opened the packet of information Elle had called her "gift." As I read through the pages of transcriptions of phone conversations and meetings, emails, and texts between Carlotta and her sister, her sister and other attorneys concerning me and Hawk, I felt sick with regret that I'd ignored her. If only, if only, if only I'd opened it a year ago, I would have done many things differently.

Now I saw my encounters with Carlotta over the past year in a different light. I recognized how Mitch's wife had steered her conversations to get me to make statements that would set me up for a conflict of interest. Now I understood her references to things she said happened but in fact never had. Carlotta referred to estate planning sessions she and Mitch had with me. But Carlotta had never been to my office with Mitch. I hadn't corrected her memory of these things; I thought stress was confusing her thoughts. In hindsight, I realized she was setting me up. If only I hadn't ignored Elle Hawk, my life would be different today.

Six months after I'd retrieved the "gift" from my trunk, my youngest son called me at the office, he sounded upset, and asked me to come home right away. I wanted to know what was so important, but all he would say is it had something to with his mother. I pressed him, and he said, "Mom left her phone here when she brought us home after ball practice. She acted a little disconnected. I think you need to take a look at something that I found on her cell before she remembers where she left it and comes back. I don't want to read it to you."

My wife, my high school sweetheart, the mother of my sons, had moved out of our home two weeks earlier. She said she needed space and that she was going to go stay with her mother and leave the boys with me for a while. Even though we were having some problems and she seemed depressed, her decision came as a shock. When she left, I thought it was spur of the moment decision.

I left the office immediately. When I walked in the door, my sons were stretched out on the sofa watching television. They both played baseball and football for their high school, practiced every afternoon, and they smelled like boys who needed a hot shower. I started to say something, but the look on my youngest son's face kept me quiet on the hygiene matter.

"I think I understand better what's been going on with Mom." He handed me his mother's phone. It was so warm that I wondered if he'd been holding it in his hand since he called. "I think Mrs. Stone has been messing with her mind for a long time."

I scrolled back and forth, looking at the text messages between my wife and Carlotta Stone. I saw that Carlotta began texting her while Mitch was in hospice, and the texting and phone calls had gone on since. I had no idea they were friends. I looked at my wife's calendar and found she and Carlotta regularly met for lunch.

From the texts, I got a real good idea how Carlotta had slowly poisoned my wife against me, convincing her that I would steal her inheritance as soon as her father died, that I was cheating on her with one of the women in my firm, that I was stealing from Mitch's trusts. Carlotta gave my wife the name of her personal physician, who could help with her anxiety. My wife had gone back to her prescription drug habit, but I had ignored the signs. Carlotta had engineered the destruction of my family.

There had been clues that my wife wasn't well and I ignored them. She often slept during the day, got angry with me over nothing. I'd chosen to put my job as Mitch's trustee, my need to help Carlotta, over my family and that was just one of the big problems the job as trustee brought me.

My second problem, a legal one, came a few weeks after I read the text messages from my wife's phone. I was in a meeting with Laura Stevens, one of the attorneys in my law firm, discussing the Stone estate, when we were interrupted by my receptionist.

"Carlotta Stone's out in the lobby and wants to speak to you now. She's not alone. A man is with her, and he looks like a lawyer to me. I'll put them in the meeting room."

Ten minutes later, I walked in to find Carlotta and her companion standing next to each looking at the river view. She was in black stretch pants, tight white top, and black high heel pumps. He looked dressed for court in a dark gray suit and red bow tie. Peter Parsons introduced himself as a member of the Rosenberg Firm and offered his hand which I shook.

I waited for either Carlotta or Parsons to start the conversation. She finally broke the silence. "I need to talk to you. It won't take long. I'm bringing Peter in to help you with the tremendous workload that is associated with my trusts. He is going to be on my team."

I didn't correct Carlotta when she referred to Mitch's trusts as hers. I'd explained several times that she was a beneficiary and that the trusts were not her personal property as she seemed to think. I let it go, as I had let go many of the incorrect statements she'd made in the past.

Carlotta laid her phone on the table. "Peter, fill him in on how things are going to work from now on? " She left the room.

I said nothing—just looked at Parsons and waited.He started with, "I thought Carlotta made an appointment for our meeting with you this morning. I guess there was a misunderstanding." I kept quiet.

Parsons had planned this ambush; it wasn't a misunderstanding at all. I could read it on his face.

"Mrs. Stone came to me not long after her husband died. She wanted a second opinion on the way you were handling your job as trustee. She said you have made her feel increasingly uncomfortable since her husband died and that she finds it hard to talk to you. Mrs. Stone believes you are also growing increasingly negative toward her."

My reply to him was, "Umm." I pressed my lips together and nodded. I wasn't quite sure how to respond to this unexpected turn of events.

"Mrs. Stone has asked me to tell you that she no longer wants you to communicate with her directly. You are to go through me. If Mrs. Stone has something to convey to you, I'll contact you. This request includes everyone in your legal and accounting firms."

I gave him nothing, did not respond; that in itself was a response. My cell vibrated. I looked down at the screen. Parsons stood up, mentioned the great view of the river, and asked if I had any questions. I said nothing. Carlotta breezed back into the room, "Looks like the meeting is over." She nodded toward Parsons. They walked out together, like a couple. Parsons turned and said, "I'm sure we'll be in touch *soon*."

I went into Laura Stevens's office and I gave her

a rundown on the meeting. Since Mitch's death, Laura and I had worked together on the matters of Carlotta and her children and Mitch's adult daughters. I could see it was taking a toll on her.

Laura said, "Let me repeat what you told me. Parsons has been giving Carlotta advice starting a short but unspecified amount of time after Mitch Stone died. She came today to let you know she doesn't want to speak directly to you or me or anyone in this firm. Parsons is to be the go-between."

I sighed. "You got it. I've been expecting trouble. I just didn't know from which direction it would come first."

"She's going to challenge the firm as trustee, isn't she?" Laura asked. "That's what this is about, isn't it?"

"I think it will eventually come to that. We'll have to wait and see how it unfolds. In the meantime, we need to make sure we do our job without mistakes. We made one when we did the codicil to her will."

Six months after Parsons instructed me not to speak with Carlotta directly but to go through him, the next problem showed itself. Peter Parsons' assistant hand-delivered a letter to me. His five single-spaced pages explained in great detail all of Carlotta's complaints against me since I became trustee. Parsons stated he was authorized by Mrs. Stone to file a petition to probate Mitch Stone's will and was considering a malpractice suit against me

"However," the letter stated "Mrs. Stone had authorized me to make a onetime settlement offer before I take any action. I will not file for probate if you turn over to Mrs. Stone, free of trust, a lump sum of twenty-five million dollars in cash and marketable securities from the Stone trusts." He gave me ten days to decide.

Another unexpected problem arose when I handed his letter to Laura. As she read the demands and threats, she turned pale, and her voice quivered when she spoke. "We need to settle this now."

I hadn't expected her to cave. I figured she would be mad as hell and want to fight. For several days, Laura argued with me about my reasons for refusing the offer. She wanted me to settle so "we can get on with our lives." But I wasn't about to fold to blackmail.

I realized Laura was the weak link, and if I couldn't manage her fears, it was going to be a big problem for me. She was a smart lawyer, worked hard, wrote brilliants briefs, but was an inexperienced fighter. She'd spend hundreds of hours dealing with Carlotta Stone and Mitch's daughters, all three of them demanding and spoiled women, and I wondered if they had worn her out or if she was simply weak.

Laura had not been raised in the same way as Stone's children. Everything she had gotten in life she'd earned. I thought when I hired her that her determination and grit to get ahead would make her strong, but the thought of losing what she'd worked so hard for had instead made her fearful.

Laura's husband became anxious when Laura told him about the problems at work. At first she kept her worries to herself and then the stress started wearing her down. Her husband worked for a financial planner but wasn't happy and was thinking about becoming a CPA. He had talked to me about it. If Laura lost her law license, they would be in big financial trouble. I felt he was encouraging Laura to pressure me to settle.

Two days before the ten day deadline was up, I told Laura that I'd notified Parsons I was not going to negotiate. I asked her to send Parson's demand letter to the beneficiaries, along with a letter from our firm stating we declined the offer. "I'd like you to call Mitch's daughters and let them know we've hired outside legal counsel to represent us in this matter and suggest they hire their own attorney. Assure them they can still call here anytime with questions or concerns about what's going on."

Laura handed me a sheet of legal size paper. "I've documented the ways Carlotta has violated the no-contest clause. I think we should threaten to invoke the no-contest clause; it would give us leverage and we could force Parsons to start a new negotiation on our terms."

I reminded her, "Negotiation would be going against the conditions of the trust. Mitch made it clear, if Carlotta violated the conditions of the trust, she gets kicked out, If one of Mitch's daughters disagrees with my position, I would have to take the matter to the trust protector, and she would never agree with negotiation."

"We can get around the trust protector. I have a good working relationship with Mitch's daughters, talk to them once a month, at least. I approve their extra spending. I'm sure they'd be on board with settlement. As for the lawyer acting as guardian of the estate for Piper and Milo, I think he will go along too. I'll speak with all of them and if they agree, I say we negotiate."

I said I would think about it. When I stopped the negotiation, I suspected Parson's would file a malpractice against me. That's what I would if I wanted to soften up another lawyer.

A week later, as I left my house for my early morning daily run down to the river park, over the big dam bridge to North Little Rock, and back, the next problem reared up. I'd lost ten pounds since my wife left me, and my running times had improved. I'd gotten used to my sons living with me every other week, and I hardly ever saw my ex. I'd found a new rhythm in my life and liked it. I felt like I did when I was a Marine, fit and strong. I was on the upswing—and now this.

I stepped out on my front porch, performed a series of stretches, and ran down the steps. Standing there with a summons in his hand was Lewis Davis, the same process server Elle Hawk had encountered outside the courtroom.

"You could have brought those to my office. You trying to ruin my day before it gets started?" I shook my head. "Can't believe you're out of bed this time of morning."

"Maybe I hadn't gone to bed yet, WP. It was a full moon—I think." He snickered and took a pack of cigarettes out of his shirt pocket. "I was instructed to serve you at home before you went for your morning run." He handed me the summons.

"If Worth was still alive, I'd think he gave you those marching orders. He liked drama, didn't he?"

"He threw a lot of work my way." Davis paused to light his cigarette. "Won't miss the mean fucker, though."

Unknown to anyone at the firm where he was a partner, Worth had pancreatic cancer. His death was a surprise to them. He'd died five weeks after Elle Hawk predicted he wouldn't live six.

I didn't bother to look at the summons. I knew it was the malpractice complaint against me that Parson had threatened to file. I opened the front door and laid the papers on the floor and headed for the trail. I'd deal with it at the office.

Parsons didn't file the complaint himself. He was using an attorney who specialized in taking down other lawyers. Judge Leticia Graves drew the case. Graves was a black woman in her sixties. She generally had a hard time with white women and expert witnesses. She made a lot of legal mistakes and was the most overturned judge in the district. I didn't know if that was good or bad for me, but I prefer a judge who knows the law. There were a number of false statements in the complaint designed to make me and Laura look guilty and greedy. But that didn't surprise me.

Clients being sued for the first time get upset when reading a complaint that contains lies and ask how that can happen. I tell them that in a civil suit, defendants are considered guilty until they prove themselves innocent. It is the opposite of criminal cases—where the defendant is considered innocent until proved guilty. The civil court assumes the charges are fact. Over time, it seemed to me, lies in civil complaints have become the norm in Arkansas.

An aging attorney from Ohio once told me he thought lawyers in Arkansas practiced Hillbilly Law. He gave as an example the number of civil complaints filled with lies and no accountability. He said the state license plates on cars should read, *Arkansas—The Land of Hillbilly Lawyering,* instead of—*The Natural State*.

I'd never been sued for malpractice, and when I read the complaint, which contained several bold lies, I found myself taking it personally, like my clients. That old saying,"until you have walked in my shoes" has a lot of truth in it.

False statement number one in the complaint stated that I represented Mitch and Carlotta for thirteen years as a couple and individually in the roles of attorney and accountant. The fact is, I'd never represented them as a couple and could prove it.

False statement number two stated Mitch agreed to revoke his premarital agreement. The fact was, he hadn't. Ironically, before they married, Carlotta started the prenuptial war. She wanted him to sign a prenup because she would "inherit substantial wealth" when her mother died. That gave Mitch the idea that he wanted one too. I made Mitch's prenup good and tight, and Carlotta got upset over it and claimed I was deliberately putting a dark cloud over their relationship and refused to sign it. Mitch told her if he wouldn't marry her if she didn't sign—he'd signed hers, and besides, she was the one who started the war. I think that's when Carlotta's hatred of me started.

False statement number three stated I had set up various entities for Carlotta and Mitch together and they believed they each had 50 percent ownership of the businesses organized for them by me. I'd never set up any joint ownerships of business for them. That wasn't Mitch's way. He hid his business matters from her; he didn't trust many folks.

False statement number four stated Mitch told Carlotta she could have two million dollars free of trust if he had an active pilot's license when he died. Mitch's trust said in plain language if he died flying the insurance money would go into a trust. He did not state *free of trust*. The suit also claimed Mitch had an active pilot license and I refused to give her the money. Mitch did not have one. I answered the complaint and the discovery phase began.

It came out that Carlotta's many attorneys had mistakenly broken the attorney-client privilege when she thought that the guardian of the estate of Mitch's minor children worked for Carlotta. That legal misstep allowed me to subpoena documents that I otherwise couldn't have gotten. JoAnne had referred to the attorneys, accountants, and insurance brokers working for her sister as Team Carlotta. With all the various law firms and attorneys and accountants involved, it was no wonder that one of the lawyers made a mistake that hurt Carlotta's case but was a big break for me.

The malpractice against me was the kick in the butt I needed to fire up my fighting sprit a notch. The time had come to put "the noose," Mitch's word for the no-contest clause, in play. Laura disagreed. She wanted me to contact Parsons and threaten to invoke the no-contest and start a new negotiation,

In our next regular Monday meeting with the other members of my firm, Laura stood up and clapped her hands together just as we were finishing up. No-one stands up and makes a speech at these meetings. She waited until she had everyone's attention. "I want this malpractice to disappear, and now it is looking like we can make that happen. We have a negotiating tool. Right now, today, we can hash out an agreement that would satisfy Carlotta's financial needs and our legal needs. If she drops the malpractice suit, we will give her twenty-five million free of trust and she takes herself out of the trust and drops the malpractice. It will be a win for all parties. Who agrees with me?"

"The wild card here is that trust protector. She is an obstacle to any kind of negotiation we enter into with Parsons. What about her?" That came from our most junior partner. It surprised me he spoke.

"We can get around that road block," Laura explained how that could be done. To my surprise, with the exception of the new member, the rest agreed with her. They feared I would lose the malpractice and the firm would close. I agreed to think about it until our next Monday meeting. What they thought mattered, but the decision belonged to me. Mutiny—that's what I was looking at.

After a lot of soul searching, using my "devil's advocate" method, I decided to go along with Laura's plan and negotiate. It would make my life a whole lot easier. If Hawk objected, I didn't know if she would try to do anything about it if the other beneficiaries agreed with me. I called Parsons and set up a meeting at my office. After a little over four hours, the three of us came away with terms we could live with, and Parsons made the appointment with the mediation service. Five days later, I received an email from Elle Hawk.

WP—Yesterday, I called you to let you know I had learned that you had a meeting with Peter Parsons at your office. You told me it was a pre-meeting for the purpose of scheduling a mediation to negotiate a settlement with Carlotta regarding her violations of Mitch's no-contest clause. I am writing to go on record and to remind you that Mitch did not specify mediation if the clause was violated. In our telephone conversation yesterday, you told me these things.

-Carlotta is in violation of the no-contest, but you don't want to file a lawsuit to have her removed as beneficiary because it would be expensive tax wise and in legal fees.

-You said you were worried that Carlotta would team up with the other beneficiaries and challenge the trusts. You felt they had a good chance to win based on a couple of Arkansas laws. It was a worry to you that Carlotta had information from Mitch's computer and cell phones, and you couldn't predict the outcome of that information.

I disagree with you for the following reasons.

-Mitch would not care how much it cost in taxes or legal fees to kick Carlotta out if she violated the no-contest. He made it clear he wanted the clause enforced. He did not specify negotiation. He wanted removal.

-Mr. Doyle, as you know, is the undisputed expert in trust law in Arkansas. He examined Mitch's estate plan after you drew it up. He is not worried about the laws you cited that you think could overturn Mitch's trust if the beneficiaries ganged up on you.

-You have known since before Mitch died that Carlotta had all the info from his computer and his cell phone and you have never said it concerned you. Now you say it

worries you. Are you worried she knows something that will hurt Mitch or will hurt you?

Mediation means negotiation. As trustee, you cannot override any part of Mitch's trusts without the approval of the trust protector. Your job as trustee is to carry out Mitch's intentions in his trusts. The trust protector's job is to agree or not agree to the changes you want to make.

This path you have taken looks like an attempt to change Mitch's intentions in his trusts without passing it by the trust protector. You disappoint me, and I think Mitch would feel betrayed.

Elle Hawk

I showed the email to Laura. She asked if I was going to cancel the mediation. I said I didn't know if Elle Hawk could do anything unless one of the beneficiaries broke ranks. We decided to keep the mediation date.

"Kelpe!"

Laura always called me WP and she'd never used that tone with me. For a second I thought I was imagining it and turned toward her.

"Doyle will pursue this for Elle. Everything she has intervened in to block Carlotta, he has won for her. I didn't think the judge would let Hawk intervene when Carlotta wanted to be named financial guardian of her own kids, but the judge allowed it. Then the judge ruled against Carlotta and he appointed a guardian for her kids. I get why Carlotta is so obsessed with her. If I had kids, and my mother-in-law kept me from having the right to make financial decisions for them, I will would want to kill her too."

"Laura! Go home and get some rest. I'm going to forget what you just said." It sounded to me like she hated Elle as much as Carlotta did. My tone made it clear she had crossed a line.

She seemed to sway and suddenly looked tired out to me. When she spoke her voice sounded shaky, "I'm sorry, WP. I just don't like the emotions and drama in this case; it's messy and ugly. I'm just so sorry. Don't worry about me, really, I'm fine."

Three days later, both Peter Parsons and I received correspondence from Clarence Doyle. He stated he represented Elle Hawk as trust protector and proceeded to give the legal reasons mediation was not an option. His message was clear and concise and left no doubt I was going down the wrong path.

—Carlotta's filings against the will and the trust constitute an objection to the distribution directive under the trust.

—Kelpe can only deviate from the distribution directive with the trust protector's approval. Mediation is a deviation. The trust protector would have to approve mediation. Her decision is binding on the trustee and beneficiaries. Therefore —no mediation should occur.

I handed Doyle's letter to Laura. "Elle Hawk just officially blew the mediation out of the water. I have no choice but to immediately file to invoke the no-contest clause. Doyle is right. I can't go through mediation without her approval; it doesn't matter what the beneficiaries want."

"What can Elle do? Trust protectors are just tie breakers. Let's sit tight and see if Doyle does anything except write letters."

I repeated, "Doyle is right. Face it. Mediation is a deviation and it isn't an option unless the trust protector agrees. We knew that but decided to ignore it. We chose to think of her only as a tie breaker and hoped Doyle wouldn't get involved. I need to get out in front of this and try to save some face."

"But!" I interrupted her. "This is what's going to happen. I'm filing to invoke the no-contest tomorrow. Period!"

"Looks like I don't have a say and my ass is on the line along with yours. I wouldn't be in this malpractice suit if it weren't for you."

"Wrong. It was your decision. As soon as Mitch died, you came to me and outlined the role you wanted to play as one of the trustees and you sold me on how you would be better for the job than other members of the firm. You're not a victim. You've put in a lot of hours and were paid for every one of them."

She stood there and looked at me, no expression, and I walked away, before she could speak, if she was even going to. I hoped Parsons was suffering as he read Doyle's letter. It was his job to inform Carlotta that Elle Hawk had won another round. I figured she was already planning how she was going to spend her twenty-five million. When Parsons took that away from her, Carlotta would explode. If that didn't do it, when she found out I'd invoked the no-contest, she would go ballistic.

In a way, I was relieved. I was starting to feel like a traitor, a coward, going into negotiations, giving Carlotta what I knew Mitch wouldn't want. I didn't know why I even considered taking the easy way out. I wondered if I was too influenced by Laura Stevens and her fears, or if dealing with this trust was wearing me thin and I was tired. Trust work is not for me. I know that now.

I also had to face the fact that Elle Hawk was Mitch's shogun, not me. In ancient Japan, I would have had to commit seppuku to restore my honor and the honor of my family for disloyalty to the emperor. In the Marines, I would be guilty of treason.

Mitch knew if I couldn't control the situation, it was up to the trust protector to come through for him. Mitch had read the whole thing right.

CHAPTER 14— CARLOTTA STONE

Peter Parsons' personal assistant asked me to stop by the office around eleven that morning. I worried the news was bad, but maybe it was way too good to give over the phone. Maybe Elle Hawk had been attacked by a shark out in Hawaii and bled to death on the beach. I took a moment to imagine that. The last time she was in Little Rock I'd paid plenty to have her taken care of and what happened—some kind of mess up that was never fully explained. The Mongoose Firm I paid to take care of her slipped up and now she was still causing me trouble. I did not get my big ass deposit back and I wanted to object, but my contact told me to leave it alone—it wasn't the kind of business you could complain to the better bureau about. I asked what the requested visit was about, but the personal assistant didn't know.

It'd been a while since we'd met at Peter's office. I took quite a bit of time to select my outfit for our face-to-face. Not black, even though it's my favorite color. Mitch had been dead three years by now, I was moving on with my life, and that included dressing in something other than black or beige.

The curse of Elle Hawk suddenly came into my mind—again. *So go enjoy your empty future . . .* Those words kept popping up more and more as the malpractice suit against WP dragged along. I reached for the little brown bottle of mood magic, tossed back the pink pill, and washed it down with my Diet Coke. I ran my hands down the line of garments in my closet room.

The space was all mine now; no more sharing it with Mitch. I pulled out my Oscar de La Renta off-white blouse from the hanger, selected my new deep-blue Gucci skirt, and stepped into a pair of Prada pumps. I started to pull back my hair into a low ponytail but decided to let it flow. I'd just had my color refreshed the day before and my lashes rewoven. I put on my favorite pair of dangling diamonds and applied pink lipstick. I looked in my full-length mirror and liked how I looked.

I arrived at the office fifteen minutes late and blamed it on the traffic. Truth was, I forgot where I was going and had to turn around. I wondered if I'd taken two of the happy pills instead of one, but my head was feeling clearer since I stopped at Starbucks for a quad espresso and a biscotti.

Peter came out to reception and walked me back to his office, like he had on our first meeting. I thought he looked thinner than the last time I saw him and hoped he wasn't going to get sick and die on me like Jim Worth had. I asked him about himself and his family but didn't really listen to what he said. I already knew how his wife was doing. We were in the same yoga class, and we often had coffee together afterwards. We were becoming friends. Peter's wife didn't know my last name was Stone, and in our yoga class, I called myself Mackie.

Parsons got down to business as soon as he shut the door to his office. I was glad we weren't in the conference room with his assistant taking notes. I wondered why we were back to the more personal. He laid a stack of papers on the table between us and said, "I'm surprised at something that just happened. Kelpe filed a petition regarding the *in-terrorem* clause in Mitch's trust. The case is in Wendell Graham's court."

"The terrorism clause is what?" I didn't have a clue what he meant. "That judge wasn't he in the paper recently about some kind of black thing? He's a . . . a black man isn't he?"

"Yes, he was on the front page. He is an activist, very smart, a preacher too, used to be an appeals court judge but wasn't re-elected due to his activism. He worries me for many reasons but most of all because he was the judge who ruled in Elle Hawk's favor when her step-daughters challenged her as Beck trustee and the trust had a no-contest clause like Mitch's trust does. It went to the Arkansas Supreme Court and Graham's decision was upheld. Basically, Kelpe's asking the judge to decide if you have violated the no-contest clause."

It seemed he was always explaining the trusts or other legal matters to me. I couldn't tell if he thought I couldn't understand or if this was just his way of always being in control. At this moment, my mind was so fuzzy, I really couldn't think. But the words black and preacher stuck in my mind. I could see him hanging on my tree.

I leaned in toward Peter. I could smell the wintergreen mint on his breath. I said, "But I didn't challenge the trust—you told me that. You said Kelpe would give up and settle with me when you filed the malpractice, and I would walk away with twenty-five million free and clear of Mitch."

"Try not to worry. You haven't challenged anything. Kelpe is saying that you have, but there is no proof and he has to prove it to Judge Graham, and he cannot. Look at this as another move in a chess game."

"I don't understand what's happening. We were going to negotiate with him, and now he has suddenly filed that thing like a lawsuit against me."

"Stick with me. I will go over the chronology of what we've done so far. First, we asked Kelpe to negotiate with us—he agreed. But Elle Hawk found out, her attorney stepped in, and then Kelpe withdrew from the negotiation. In response to Kelpe quitting the negotiation, we filed the malpractice against him. When we did that, he claimed you violated the no-contest. Right now, we are no longer in any negotiations with Kelpe. The bottom line is Graham will decide if you violated the no-contest clause. After that happens, we will take the next step. Do you understand?"

"I get it. What else? I have a feeling more is on your mind."

"Kelpe has cut off your monthly allowances and other distributions from the trust. He is putting them in a special account until the no-contest problem is solved. The Kelpe firm will no longer be taking care of paying your household and other bills for you."

I thought I was going to faint. I could go broke before all this got settled, if Peter didn't get off his ass and fix it. That thought scared me. I needed to find out how much I had in my personal checking account. I hadn't had to write a check in so long, I didn't even know where I'd put the check book.

I asked for a Diet Coke to settle my nerves. "Why didn't you call or email me all this bad news? I'm so upset, I don't know if I can drive home. Didn't you think you should have warned me and given me a chance to think before making me come here?"

"It was too complicated for an email or phone call. I thought we needed to talk in person. Communication, for me anyway, is more efficient with the natural flow of the back and forth of a conversation."

“There is such a thing as Skype. I could be safe in my own house right now if you’d thought of that. I just hope I can get myself home without passing out and having a wreck.”

Peter acted like I hadn’t said a word. “Carlotta there’s another matter we need to talk about. *Arkansas Business Magazine* is planning a feature on greedy lawyers and trusts, and your malpractice against Kelpe will be one of the several examples. Now that Kelpe has filed the no-contest the writer will include that information.”

“How would a reporter know anything about what’s going on with Mitch’s trust?”

“Anything that’s filed in court is public knowledge. For instance, a reporter can go online to the Pulaski Clerk website, put in your name, and find all kinds of documents concerning you, including things like citations for dangerous driving, DUI, and lawsuits with you as plaintiff or defendant.”

“That means everyone in town could know my business. I don’t believe it.”

“The feature will be favorable to the clients and not the lawyers based on what the reporter said. This will be good for your malpractice against him if it goes to a jury. Listen, do not speak with a reporter if one calls you—anything you say could be misunderstood or twisted. Let me handle it."

Peter handed me a copy of the no-contest thing. He wanted to go over it with me. I flipped through the 172 pages.

I scanned my copy looking for something written in plain language that I could understand. My eyes found the line "Background" and I started reading and only half-listened to him.

-Mr. and Mrs. Stone married on 2-22-03. He was 36 and she was 30.
-She was his third wife and he her second husband.
-Both signed a premarital agreement and both were represented by separate council.
-Mr. Stone was involved in a successful business. She bought $62,400 to the marriage.
-Mr. and Mrs. Stone had significant marital difficulties during the marriage, regarding, among other things, Mrs. Stone's spending.
-Mr. Stone tried to keep her on budget but generally failed.-Mr. Stone was concerned about ensuring that all his children were provided for.
-Mr. Stone believed he needed a strong estate plan to manage these strong family dynamics.
-Mr. Stone was concerned about Mrs. Stone challenging provisions regarding management of assets and distribution to her and specifically included the in-terrorem provisions.
-Mr. Stone anticipated and planned for Mrs. Stone's refusal to accept her restricted access to the trusts.
-Mrs. Stone began attacking the plan with the goal of receiving as much of Mr. Stone's estate as she could free of trusts administration

I stood up and threw the papers at him. "This is a pile of shit." I waved my hand over the papers now on the floor. I raised my voice, and he could tell by the look on my face I meant it when I screamed, "You've fucked up my life! This is your fault!"

Peter opened the door and asked his assistant to come inside. I guess I scared him and he didn't know what was about to happen.
He'd never seen this side of me before. One of the other attorneys heard the commotion and followed the assistant in.

"Get them out of here. This is between us."

"No, Carlotta it isn't. This whole firm represents you. Please take a moment. I feel that Mr. Polk here," he touched a tall thin older man on the shoulder, "can help me help you understand what's going on. It isn't a catastrophe. This is the law. It takes twists and turns. Kelpe has to prove you violated the clause. He cannot do it."

Peter looked at his assistant. "You and Mrs. Stone go into the break room for a few minutes. Give Mr. Polk and me some time." He asked me how that sounded.

I walked down the hall to what looked like a small kitchen and ate two doughnuts and drank a mug of hot chocolate. When I came back, Mr. Polk said I should relax. He said he had known my dad and told me a story about them hunting down in Stuttgart. That made me feel safe. After a while I calmed down and apologized for being rude. I didn't mean it, but I had to play the game.

An hour or so later, I left their office feeling pretty good. I liked Mr. Polk, that he knew my family, that he would take care of me.

I found myself lost in thought before I realized I'd driven past the street to my house and was heading toward Pinnacle Mountain. I'd been thinking about Mitch and one of our first dates. We'd climbed Pinnacle and had a picnic there. I pulled over at The Kitchen Cafe to turn around but decided to go in and have a cheeseburger, fries, pie, a Coke. I needed comfort.

The Cafe served only organic food and the napkins were cloth, the plates were pretty and the knives and forks stainless. It had a big vegetarian menu and the only meat it served was local hamburger. It was owned by a couple from Colorado who'd moved to Little Rock a couple of years earlier. It was past lunch and the place was practically empty. I sat in a booth and faced the door. A man walked in wearing an obviously expensive black business suit and a black turban. I noticed he'd gotten out of a black Mercedes driven by a chauffeur who opened the door to the cafe for him and returned to the car.

I recognized the guy. He was famous, a psychic, he'd been on TV. I thought it must be fate that he walked in at this exact time. I'd been to Carole Tate, our local psychic, several times, but Tate knew everyone in town. This guy didn't know me at all. I was overcome with the urge to speak with him and checked my purse to make sure I had some cash. Tate charged a hundred for an hour.

The man took a seat in front of a window at a table for two. The owner appeared immediately with a pot of tea. He wasn't given a menu. It seemed to me he was expected. She came back and placed little plates of food on his table.

I watched him slowly sip his tea.

He didn't seem to be in a hurry, and I began to imagine having a session with him. It was fate. It must be fate. I left the booth and went into the ladies' room and looked at my teeth to make sure there wasn't any food between them, and rinsed my mouth, used the toilet, and went back toward my booth but bypassed it and went over to his table.

The famous man watched as I headed toward him and raised himself from his seat a little and indicated for me to sit. I did and started to speak, but he raised his hand to indicate he didn't want me to say a word. He moved his hands across the table toward me with his palms up, and I placed my hands in his. He shut his eyes and I felt my energy leave my body through my hands and enter his body. I felt my blood move, felt my eyes water, felt calm and afraid at the same time.

"Ask me the question that haunts you."

I started to explain, but he stopped me.

"Please. Just ask the question."

"Will I win?"

He withdrew his hands from mine. Shut his eyes. I waited. He opened his eyes.

"You will not win your battle against the dead man."

CHAPTER 15 —MILO STONE

Swainey, Mom's mom, dropped me off from school. I call her that because she doesn't like the word *Grandma* and her last name is McSwain. My mom walked in the house a few minutes later looking like a zombie. I asked her what was wrong and she said, "I'm taking to my bed." That's what she says when she goes to her room, shuts the door, and wants us to leave her alone.

"Here's you supper," and she sat a take-out box from The Kitchen Cafe on the counter. "Milo, baby, I've just had it with lawyers and their lying ways. Walk back to my room with me. I'm beat."

I hadn't seen her look like that since the day Dad died. I asked what was wrong.

"You know a little bit about what's going on about Mr. Kelpe trying to keep us from getting our money. Now my lawyer says Mr. Kelpe has filed a lawsuit in court and is going to kick me out of the trust. I just found out. Then I ran into a psychic who finished ruining my day. I'm beat. Oh, I think I left the car running. Will you go check on it for me." She gave me a hug and dropped backward on her bed with her clothes on.

I walked outside to the garage and found Mom's car running. I turned it off and saw a folder and picked it up and took it into the house. I opened up the takeout and started on my hamburger. I couldn't help myself, I looked in the folder and there was the lawsuit mom told me about. I took my food and the folder into my room and shut the door.

After I finished reading it, I went to the Pulaski County Clerk's website and put in her name. There were a lot of entries, and I went to every one of them and read about the lawsuits. They said awful things about Mom, Mr. Kelpe, and Gran. There is something called exhibits and there was a lot of extra information in them. I think exhibits are evidence. I need to learn more about that.

Anyway, I saw this text that Gran sent Mom after Dad died. It was Exhibit 10, and it sticks in my mind. There was over a hundred pages of transcripts of Mom's secret recording. In one of them she asked one of her lawyers, "What would happen if Elle Hawk were to suddenly die?" and he told her not to say things like that. I bet Mom wished she hadn't had a specialist take her secret recording and transcribe them. Now, Mr. Kelpe was using them against her. I didn't figure this out right away, even though I have a really high IQ. It took me a while. Mom had outsmarted herself. I thought about all my secret recordings of the neighbors and wondered if they would come back to haunt *me*.

I was going to tell Piper what was going on but decided not to because she might tell Mom I'd been snooping. I'd learned about spying from Mom, and secret recording on a cell phone, and lying. Mom is a great liar. Sometimes when I know she's lying, I believe her. I got my notebook and started a list of words to look up. One of my hobbies is making up stories. My notebooks are filled with ideas and new words. I want to write a Netflix series.

I sometimes miss Gran and the fun we always had when she visited. I miss her sister Izzy too. She has a really fast boat on the river and a talking parrot and a really cool house. Dad and I started spending more time with her after Uncle Max died. But when good thoughts about Gran come, I erase them and remind myself to hate her. Auntie Birdie and I had lots of fun too, but Mom won't let us see her either.

We haven't seen any of Dad's clan since he died. Mom won't let us go to the annual Stone family Christmas party or go to their fish fries at Uncle Ronny's farm, or do any of the things with anyone from Dad's side like we used to do. Mom kicked them out of our life.

I downloaded the filings from the Pulaski Clerk site and saved them to a folder. Then I called Clifton, my friend who lived down the street, and asked him to come over. I wanted something to do and we always found an adventure. His mom let him come because Mom was home. Home, yes—conscious, no.

While I waited, I made a video with Mom's head hanging over the side of the bed, a long string of spit dribbled out of her mouth. She was so still, I wondered if she was dead, but then she snorted and jerked and opened her eyes and spoke.

"Milo, honey, go and get me a Diet Coke." I got that on video too. It was great. I went to the kitchen, but when I got back she was under the covers, snoring.

I was nine when my dad died and now I'm almost thirteen. I'm the shortest of the boys my age and some of the girls are taller than me too, but I'm not a midget or a dwarf. I hope to make it to medium height by the time I get out of high school. Being the smartest in my class makes up for being the shortest boy.

I don't have many memories of Dad, but I do remember some of the things he told me. "Milo, when you're a short guy, the most important thing in the world is to learn to out think everyone else. Tall people try to rule the world." I keep a notebook where I write down everything I remember about Dad's advice about life.

My friend Clifton and I have a YouTube series going where we play detective, and we're up to almost two hundred followers. As detectives, we explore the Heights, spy on the people, and secretly video them. If they're doing something funny or fighting, we upload it. We don't use our own names or show our faces. If Clifton's mom found out she would take away his phone, his laptop, all his toys. She keep tabs on how much time Clifton spends on the internet, the sites he visits, and looks at his texts. My mom doesn't check up on me.

Mom doesn't know about our YouTube videos, but my big sister Piper does, and sometimes she threatens to tell Mom if I don't do what she wants. But now that Piper started having boyfriends she isn't so interested in me. I made a couple of videos of her and her boyfriends kissing in Mom's bed, and now I have something on her.

Clifton came in with his GoPro on his head so I put mine on. I told him the other day I was going down the steps and I noticed one of the panels on the wall looked funny. I never pay any attention to them because behind the panels is just a space under the house that smells musty. Last time I went in there was way before Dad got sick.

We started filming as we walked out of my room, going down the steps. I pushed the corner of the panel and it opened inward and turned on my cell flashlight and shined it around the walls.

I heard the breath go out of Clifton when the light hit on a big tree in the middle of the room. I almost screamed at the sight of the dolls hanging from nooses off the branches. It looked like the same tree that's in Swainey's backyard down in Lonoke, only smaller.

I examined the dolls, but he stepped back from the tree, "They've got real hair on them, and clothes, and some of the faces look like people I know." I snapped pics of each one with my cell while Clifton scanned the scene with his GoPro.

I touched the dolls, but Clifton didn't. I saw Dad hanging and wondered if voodoo had killed him, but I knew better. Dad's uncle DeWight had been hit by a car and died—his doll was hanging there. I saw Aunt Shelly, my stepsisters, and people I didn't know. I was glad Clifton was with me. If I'd been alone, I might have run and not explored.

Clifton whispered, "Let's get out of here. This is way creepy." But he didn't move; he kept on filming. Then he said he thought we got it all and turned to leave.

"Wait. That's Mom's yoga pad under the tree. Voodoo Yoga—let's look that up."

We ran up the steps and went immediately to my room. Clifton wanted to go to his house, and I didn't want to stay in mine, so we left, When we got to Clifton's, I smelled cooking and my stomach rumbled even though I'd had that big burger my mom left for me. In my house, cooking smelled like Chinese takeout or pizza. Clifton's mom was frying chicken. I had never seen Mom do that, but I remember sometimes Dad fried it and made gravy and mashed potatoes.

"I'll fix you boys a snack," and then she took a hard look at Clifton. "Honey, just what have you two been up to?" She took Clifton's face in her hands said that he looked pale, and she hoped he wasn't coming down with something. "Go. I'll bring snacks." We went to his room and watched the video and looked at the still shots.

And then I had a great idea. We looked up voodoo practices, wrote a script, and uploaded *Voodoo Yoga in the Heights* to YouTube. It went viral—my dream come true.

CHAPTER 16 —PETER PARSONS

I was still reeling from my last encounter with Carlotta Stone when one of my partners brought in his cell. “Take a look at this.” I watched Voodoo Yoga in the Heights. I saw my image on a hanging doll. I recognized the stylized mat with the name Chloe spelled out in yoga poses. That could mean my wife is in a class with the person who owns this tree.

Then my colleague said his wife thought she recognized the carpet on the steps and thought this was the Stone’s house but wasn’t sure. This meant Sylvia probably knows Carlotta. I had heard gossip that Kelpe’s personal life had fallen apart after he became trustee. I had a noose around my neck and Kelpe did too and we were hanging on the tree. I had to sit down.

“Looks like you’ve been lynched,” my partner teased. I didn’t laugh, and he said, “Sorry, it’s not funny.”

My phone pinged a text from my wife. Sylvia sent a link and asked me to look at it and call her and I did.

Sylvia started talking right away. “Can you believe this shit. When I got to class, everyone was talking about the YouTube. Chloe was beside herself because her signature mat was under the tree. All of us were trying to figure out whose tree it was and some recognized the dolls. Do you think this is one of your clients? I know that sounds crazy, but why else would you be lynched?"

Sylvia didn't give me a chance to answer before starting up again. "One of the women in class thought this could be a video a competitor did to ruin Chloe's business. She thinks they got a tree, put dolls on it, set the scene, and photoshopped Chloe's mat in to make it look like this was her personal yoga room."

"What's the name of the woman who said that?" I had a feeling she was going to answer "Carlotta Stone."

"Her name is, Mackie. She told Chloe she was probably being stalked. It freaked her out so bad she cancelled our yoga class."

I knew Carlotta's maiden name was McSwain and it wasn't a stretch to figure she was Mackie. I asked how long Mackie had been in yoga with her, and my wife said a little over two years and that she had gotten to know her, and they usually went to coffee with friends after class was over.

After I hung up with Sylvia, I turned to my parter, "Call your wife right now and tell her not to tell anyone she thinks this video was taken at Carlotta Stone's house." I listened to his end of the conversation and could tell there was a problem as soon as he hung up.

"My son and Milo Stone made the video and put it on YouTube. My wife said last night they looked like they were up to something. This morning, when she saw the YouTube, she became suspicious because she thought one of the boy detectives sounded a little like Milo. She went in Clifton's room and looked at what was on his GoPro. He had it with him last night when he and Milo got back to our house. My wife confronted him and he lied, and then he admitted it."

My associate asked me what I was going to do about it. I didn't have an answer because what could I do?

I was glad it was the end of a long week by the time this day ended. On Fridays after work, I usually stop at the BirdDog Bar in North Little Rock before heading home. No one I know or do work for would even think about going in there, and that's why I like it. I take off my tie and open my collar before I walk in. The place is usually half full but gets crowded as the night goes on. The owner tends bar, he knows what I drink, and he sets my drink down before I ask.

I was finishing up my Woodford when a gray-haired woman dressed in old-style Levi's, a plaid shirt, and Dingo boots came in and took a stool a couple of places from me. She ordered a shot of tequila and a beer. She seemed to fit right in: the way she looked, her demeanor, the way she sat on the barstool.

The woman leaned across the empty seats and spoke. “My name is Elle Hawk.”

My day got started with Voodoo yoga, and now the trust protector walked into the BirdDog. I was speechless and glad I hadn’t jumped when she said her name. She didn’t wait for me to speak.

“I’d like to have a few minutes with you.” She indicated a booth. “Will you sit with me?”

I didn’t want to talk to her. I needed to get out of there. I made a motion to the bartender, indicating I wanted my check.

Hawk grinned and stood up. She was a short compact woman. “I took care of it already. I was hoping to barge in on your time.” I told her I needed to get going and made a point of looking at my watch.

She reached out and touched it. “I see you wear a vintage Rolex Submariner and not one of those smart watches that counts steps and acts like a computer. Don’t worry, I’m not trying to pick you up.” She gave a little laugh but I didn’t speak.

“Don’t be scared. The bartender knows me, and I know who you are—the lawyer for my son’s widow, Carlotta. Don’t get up and run off which it looks to me like you want to do. I figure it was your idea to send that brute after me in Maui but you got Jim Worth to do your dirty work. I'm not one to hold a grudge."

I felt like I was in an episode of *Ozark* and talking to Darlene, the poppy grower.

"I'm figuring we can do a little socializing at a local bar." I didn't answer but got up to leave.

"Now come on, let's have a seat in the booth. I won't take much of your time."

I was curious about her and what she had to say. Against my better judgment, I followed her, and the bartender brought over another round.

"Mr. Parsons, Sylvia knows Carlotta Stone but she thinks her name is Mackie. The two of them have become friends. A doll that represents you is hanging from the lynching tree. You've disappointed Carlotta, and believe me, she's the kind who knows the best way to hurt someone who has let her down, or made her angry, is to destroy them and the people close to them."

Hawk stopped and waited for me to respond. But I didn't. I was trying to get over the fact that she knew about the tree and the name Mackie and that my wife's name was Sylvia. I had questions but didn't think it would be smart to show my hand by asking them. I was torn between giving in to her and getting into a conversation or doing nothing. I kept my mouth shut. So she started giving me reasons to listen.

"Look what happened to WP Kelpe's marriage when he disappointed Carlotta and she came to you. Look how you did her bidding and helped her set him up for the conflict of interest leading to a malpractice suit. You were also aware she befriended Kelpe's wife for the purpose of disrupting his marriage and look what happened to his private life. Now you're on her hit list. You probably don't believe me, but believe the tree."

I held her gaze before I spoke. I found her a little creepy. "I'm impressed, as you intended me to be. I don't understand what you want, or understand your motive, or why you even care about me which I don't believe that you do. You are trying to turn me against my client and that is your motive for being here."

"I've seen a lot of personal destruction done by Carlotta to my son, his daughters, his attorney, his father, to name a few. I'm guessing you saw the YouTube—Voodoo Yoga in the Heights; it seems everyone in town has. That you're hanging from the tree is proof she's coming after you."

"I read the text you sent to Carlotta just hours after her husband died. That was extremely cruel." I needed to control the narrative, but I was failing.

Hawk tossed back her shot and took a sip of her beer. "Oh, was it? Maybe you should get your head out of your ass and do a little investigation of the last six weeks of my son's life."

"Carlotta's told me quite a bit about you, and I understand why you frighten her. Now you're trying to scare me. It won't work." I got up to leave and put a tip on the table.

"Oh, sit down and listen. My motive in warning you to protect your family is a selfish one. The only person who has any influence with Carlotta is you, at least for now. No one in my family has seen the kids since Mitch died. He hoped some of his cousins would do things with his kids, but Carlotta won't allow it. Piper has dance, which gives her some discipline, but that's falling to the wayside now that she's had a few boy friends. Her school decided she won't be allowed to continue after this year, and she's been going there since first grade. Milo is a feral child, no supervision, roams around spying on neighbors and putting videos of them on YouTube.I could go on. I am desperate as you can see. I am here asking you to help two children who are in danger. "

I asked Hawk what she thought I could possibly do. She sounded like my mother when she answered. "You could start by giving Carlotta some personal guidance. Suggest she let Pipe and Milo see their cousins and go to the Stone fish fries—things like that. How would you feel if Milo was your son? The children are isolated from an entire support system they desperately need."

I believed she was sincere when she said, "I'm

helping you save your family because I want you to help my grandchildren. If you don't listen, I guarantee you won't be married this time next year."

Elle Hawk stood up, looked down at me, and walked away. She laid a hundred on the bar top as she passed and left. I suddenly felt ashamed of the way I'd treated her, but I didn't call her back or follow her out the door.

After a few minutes, I went to the bar for another round, not caring if I'd need an Uber. I asked the bartender if he knew Elle Hawk.

"You bet I do. We've known each other since high school. She dated my best friend, Allen Stone, and they got married right here in my dad's place two days after she turned eighteen. Allen came in regularly for the past fifty years, until he got the kidney cancer. Whenever Elle comes back to Little Rock, she stops in."

I couldn't believe the coincidence. I thought I'd found the perfect bar, a place where no one knew me, yet the bartender knew Elle Hawk and she appeared there at the same time I was having a drink. She was having me followed, that was obvious. If she was doing that, I wondered what Carlotta Stone was up to.

After what had happened this morning, I felt the urge to get home and protect my family. I was spooked. So I left the drink untouched on the bar.

As it turned out, that was a wise move. When I got home, my wife was sitting at the kitchen table reading online. My son was busy at the counter making macaroni and cheese. He was going to be a big kid and he liked to eat. When he was seven, he was already helping in the kitchen and, my wife showed him how to make his favorite things like rice with butter, or mashed potatoes, and now he was up to macaroni and cheese. His speciality was baking cookies and cakes.

From the look on Sylvia's face, I saw worry. I guess the Voodoo Yoga had really stressed her out because she usually smiled when I walked in and hugged me, but she stayed at the table and closed her laptop.

"I'm in need of a hug right now," and I came up behind her and put my arms around her shoulders and kissed her neck. She turned toward me and gave me my full body hug. I loved her size, she is two inches shorter than me and I am a few inches over six feet.

I wondered if Elle Hawk was right and Carlotta *had* gotten to her. I was only half right. After we ate macaroni with garlic bread and salad for supper and espresso cake for dessert, my wife said, "You all go play some ball. I'll do the dishes since our budding chef cooked."

My son and I went to the game room, where we have a pool table, a ping-pong table, a card table, the works. When he was born, Sylvia said she didn't want any more kids, and she was going to turn our home into a place our son's friends would want to hang out. We played several games of ping-pong and a round of pool, and then he turned on the giant television. I went looking for Sylvia and found her in our home office.

One of the things I like about my wife is that she gets to the point. Now that I had met Elle Hawk, I could see they had this in common. Sylvia stayed behind her desk, I took a seat on the on the love seat near the fire place, and she started her story.

"After Chloe canceled class, Mackie and a couple of us went to the new shop in the Heights and had coffee. When we first met Mackie, she was always a little sad because her husband died of cancer and he was only fifty and she had two young children to raise. She said yoga saved her life, and so had I and the other women in our group. Mackie has talked more often about what it was like to be a widow and to have a trust fund that was managed by a lawyer who was stingy, and who she thought was stealing from her. Her mother found her another attorney to prove she was right about the trustee and to help her get free of the trust."

Then Sylvia's demeanor changed, but only slightly. "Little by little, Mackie told us about her new attorney. He was several years younger than her and married, with a son, and they were attracted to each other. Sometimes they met for lunch or for a cocktail after work, did some flirting, but that was all. She could tell he was interested in her and it made her feel good. After about a year, they hooked up when his wife went out of town to go to a yoga retreat. They get together about once a week for what Mackie calls *date time*."

After coffee with her friends, Sylvia went to her rowing class and the gym. Later that day, she was looking through stacked-up mail and found several back issues of a local magazine that focuses on social things around town. There was an issue that had Mackie's picture on the front and it caught her attention. That's when my wife learned Mackie's real name was Carlotta Stone.

"I Googled Carlotta and Mitchell Stone and saw references to lawsuits, and I looked them up and found out all about Mackie, aka Carlotta. I went through every reference in there and saw exhibits that were transcripts of Carlotta's secret recordings of her meetings with the trustee and another lawyer at the firm. I read part of a transcript of a meeting with Carlotta, WP Kelpe, and you. It was the meeting you told Kelpe that he couldn't speak to Carlotta directly, that he had to go through you. Now, I want to know what your relationship with Carlotta Stone is all about."

The first thing I did was to ask Sylvia if she thought I was cheating with Carlotta? I was a little surprised at her answer.

"She isn't your type, too small. Second, let's

face it, you don't have a strong sex drive, so I don't see you chasing pussy around. But this is what bothers me: You went along with setting up a good man like WP Kelpe. That surprised me. I never would have expected that from you. Kelpe and my brother went to law school together, and my brother likes him. That bit makes me wonder about you, something I've never done before. Who are you?"

I felt deflated and sorry I'd ever taken on Carlotta Stone as a client. I'd had my doubts from the start, but I'd wanted her money.

Sylvia asked me if I thought that was Carlotta's tree, and I told her what went on that morning. Once I started spilling out the story, I couldn't stop. I told her about Elle Hawk and her warning, about how Carlotta had destroyed Kelpe's marriage, and how I came to take her on as a client—I needed the money. "I admit, I saw her as a cash cow and I believed that I could get her what she wanted. I regret Kelpe and my part in trying to take down his career." Getting it off my chest felt good.

The moon was coming in the window, and Sylvia said, "Do you realize that today is Friday the thirteenth; look at that full moon." She went to the bookshelf, got her Nikon, put it on a tripod, and took a series of pictures of the moon—old school, not cell phone photography. She would later print them on paper, not send them off and have them put on metal.

My vintage Rolex was made in the early nineteen sixties, and it was Sylvia's wedding present to me. Sylvia is old school, and that's one of my favorite things about her.

The moon was shinning its hot moonlight on me, and I felt exposed to Sylvia and to myself. I couldn't keep on representing Carlotta Stone unless I wanted to keep lying to myself. The lies you tell yourself, and believe, are the worst. I had a bad feeling I hadn't heard the last of this.

CHAPTER 17 — CARLOTTA STONE

I couldn't believe that my sacred room had been violated by Milo and my lynching tree put on YouTube for the world to see. I felt raped. At first, I thought I should tear it down and burn the tree and the dolls, but then my good sense took hold. I wasn't going to destroy the only room in the house I loved, besides my closet, or the lynching tree, or the dolls I'd made.

I'm not good with electric tools, but I know how to use a hammer and where Mitch kept it, and the nails. I got them and nailed the panel shut from the inside. I would get a painter to paint over those damn decorative panels and cover up the fancy wood. Then I would have the steps carpeted in another color. I went to my tree, lit scented candles, and lay down in the corpse pose under it. I was almost in total state of relaxation when I realized what I'd done—nailed myself inside, and there was no other way out.

I got the hammer and tried to pry out the nails, but they were in too deep. I started to panic and yelled for Milo and Piper, then remembered they weren't home. I reached for my phone, which was always in the side pocket of my leggings, but my cell wasn't there. I had candles and a lighter, and I thought about burning a hole in the panel, but decided that might not be a good idea. I forced myself to calm down.

I knew I would hear Milo when he came home

from wherever he was, and I could bang on the panel and he could call 9-1-1. I wouldn't starve; I had a supple of Zone bars under the tree.

I'd never explored beyond the tree room and I started looking around. There were a lot of wires and pipes on the ceiling that ran under floor of what I supposed was the kitchen, laundry room, and living room. I noticed a panel in the back wall and hit it with the hammer and it broke away. The floor behind the door was dirt. That must be what Mitch called the crawl space.

I saw a small window at the far end and had to crawl on my hands and knees over the dirt to get to it, When I got there, I looked out and saw the backyard. I opened the window, pulled myself up, and went out into the yard. All these years I lived in this house, I'd never noticed this window. This would be my new way into my sacred room. My sanctuary was safe, and I'd found a new way to get to it that no one else knew about. I would have to crawl over the dirt, but I could put down some carpet pieces to make a path.

One thing I noticed in the dirt area was that it smelled funny, kind of like a gas burner does on the stove when you turn it on but before it lights up. I could see that animals had made some nests in there and wondered if they were raccoons. I heard they have rabies. But I didn't care as long as they stayed in there and didn't get into my tree room. There were a few wires down, but I guessed they weren't important because the lights in the house worked.

The important thing was I could get back to my tree, lay down under it, and start thinking about the last few days—the no-contest lawsuit, the psychic saying I wouldn't win against the dead man, *Voodoo Yoga in the Heights*, and nailing myself inside the room. I fell asleep, and the next thing I knew, I heard Milo calling me. I crawled back over the dirt and out the window. I guess I looked pretty funny, because as soon as Milo saw me come in the house he started laughing.

I ignored the laugh and I asked Milo where he'd been, he said exploring; whatever that means. I asked him what he wanted for dinner and he said nothing. He'd walked to the McDonald's and had fries and a burger. At least he knew how to feed himself. I wondered where Piper was and Milo pointed toward her bedroom and said she was with her new boyfriend watching a movie and making out. I guess I'd been asleep under my tree for a long time for all of this to have gone on. I didn't mention his violation of my sacred space or Voodoo Yoga on YouTube.

I couldn't quit thinking about Peter Parsons and how he'd ruined my life. I liked the yoga class, but I didn't need it any more. I'd accomplished what I'd wanted to do. And then it struck me—my picture in that stupid local magazine. If Peter's wife saw it, she would know my real name. But she couldn't connect me to him, because the articles didn't mention his name. I hoped he wasn't the kind of attorney who talked about his clients outside work.

I went cold. I may have outsmarted myself. I decided I was just going to pretend she didn't read the magazine and be nicer to him from now on. Right now, he was all I had. I still couldn't shake off that the psychic had said I would lose to the dead man. Unless the famous man had read the articles and seen my picture and recognized me, he wouldn't know to say what he had. But maybe he had read them. It didn't matter. Peter had said if we lost, we could appeal. But he didn't have anything to lose; I did. We hadn't done the contingency thing and that was his idea, not mine. I guessed he probably decided to stick with our original agreement because he needed the steady money or he didn't have faith in our case.

My sister suggested to me, when he chose to stick with fee based, I should have stopped trying to break free of the trust, made peace with Kelpe, and learn to live with Mitch's estate plan. She told me stubbornness was my downfall, and I said I was determined and that was a strength. She suggested I get a dictionary and look up the difference. My mother had agreed with her, and I got mad at both of them.

Now that my mind had cleared, I knew what I needed to do: remove the dolls and everything else and disassemble the tree, clear out the room like nothing had been in there. Then I would have a carpenter come in and make an opening to the room from the back of the closet in Shelly's old room. That way I wouldn't have to crawl over the dirt when I put the tree back. I'd have the hallway and the panels painted a different color. I'd noticed in the video that I could see the corner of an oil painting of my house, and I'd move that, and have the steps re-carpeted.

I waited until Monday to get started because the kids were in and out all weekend. Mr. Handyman Inc. said they would send over a carpenter on Tuesday. I figured it would take all day Monday to wrap up the dolls and put them in individual boxes, and take apart the tree and put it back in the crates it came in, and then I'd go pick out carpet and schedule the installation. I felt like a Realtor again, staging a house for sale. That gave me the idea of getting back in the business. That was how I met Mitch, and it had made me a rich woman, if I could get my hands on what I deserved as a wife.

When the handyman came, he threw me a curveball. I told him that I wanted a door into the storage area from the back of the closet so I wouldn't have to come in through the window. He asked me why I'd nailed the entry panel shut, and I said I didn't, my husband did, because he didn't want the children to go in there. He said it would be easy to release the panel and not tear into the closet, but I said I wanted him to do it my way.

Then he said my house was in a dangerous situation, and I told him about the home security system, the cameras, and he just gave me a blank stare and said, "Ma'am, that situation under you house is putting you in danger, not prowlers. There are vermin down there who have made nests and chewed the insulation from the electrical wires. Some of the wires are on the ground, and the gas pipes and water lines are leaking. I smelled gas as soon as I got under there."

He showed me the window I had come through to get under the house and said it was eaten up with dry rot and he could see where it leaked. It scared me a bit when he said, "If we get a good rain, and the water runs under the house in that area and pools, and the exposed wires are on the ground, and the water hits them, they'll spark, and with the gas leaks, your house will most likely explode."

I focused on the words "most likely," that was the operative phrase, and I asked him if he would go ahead and put in the door behind the closet, get started on the painting and when I got back from vacation, he could fix the other stuff. He said he wouldn't do the work until the problems were solved. He told me I needed a licensed plumber and electrician and a pest control company to remove the animals that were nesting in and under the house. "Ma'am, If I lived here, I would stay someplace else until the problems are fixed."

I couldn't believe it. I didn't want the house to burn down because I owned it outright. If Judge Graham said I was out of the trust, I could get a loan on it. I couldn't do that while I was in the trust because it was forbidden. I could probably sell it for around nine hundred thousand. I would get the things done when I got back.

I kept wondering about Peter. I thought about calling and asking him if there was anything I needed to do to get ready for the hearing—just ask him anything so I could get a feel for him but decided to do nothing. Best to let a little time pass when you've had a big blow up.

As it turned out, Peter called me the day before we left for Aspen to wish me a happy holiday and so on. He sounded like himself, telling me to have a good time, and not to worry about the court, and suggesting a new restaurant in Aspen that he and his wife enjoyed. So I guess I was worried about nothing, and that made me feel better. I could tell he didn't know about the Mackie-was-aka-Carlotta thing, or he wouldn't have been so sweet. Looked like I dodged a bullet. I've always been lucky that way. The kids and I would have the best time ever in Aspen, and I hoped it wouldn't be our last time to take a private jet.

When we got back home two weeks later, the lights were on, the dogs were fine, and the heat was working. I'd go ahead and call Mr. Handyman so they could send out the plumber and electrician. But now that I had that checked off my list, a new irritation arose. I heard that the trust protector was on her way to Little Rock for the no-contest hearing. I wondered if I could stop her. I didn't have my tree to meditate under and help me come up with ideas, so I took to my bed.

CHAPTER 18 — ELLE HAWK

Five weeks before I ambushed Peter Parsons at the BirdDog, I walked out of the house I'd lived in for thirty years, put my two mini Doxies in carriers and boarded the red eye to the mainland. Maui had become a one-dimensional life for me. Back in the mid-nineteen seventies, my mother moved to Oahu because she needed a new life, but she only lasted there a year. I've lasted over thirty in a place Harvey and I came to when we wanted a new life. I locked my door and left Maui. I'd be back one of these days, just didn't know when.

I arrived at LAX and took a taxi to the nearest BMW dealership, where I bought a used SUV with ten thousand miles on it. I planned to meander to Cincinnati, taking a month or so to go wherever whim took me. Both of my daughters had married men from Ohio and moved there and raised their children. Birdie, my oldest daughter, had lived there twenty-eight years and my younger daughter, Ginny, who used to live in Maui, moved to Cincinnati eighteen years ago. She'd married a friend of her sister's husband and they had two teenagers—boy and a girl.

A few months after Harvey died, I bought a two-story house across the street from Birdie in a well-kept, older neighborhood where the houses were built in the nineteen thirties. I let Birdie and Ginny use it to operate their business, an Airbnb they named *The Buffalo Inn.* They decorated it with their father's collection of

American Indian art that included sculptures and paintings, a buffalo head, a deer pelt, handmade oak bookcases with glass fronts; a wooden icebox served as a television stand, and the twelve-foot-long antique oak library table fit just right in the dining room.

I stay there when I'm in Cincinnati and pay them rent even though I own the place. I enjoy the over-the-top look of animal heads and hides. Harvey wouldn't have liked it at all. He was fussy about decor. Now that Harvey is dead and gone, I can't imagine even hooking up with a man again, needing his opinion on the color of the walls or the furniture I choose. Dogs are perfect.

I didn't mention to Birdie or Ginny that I was driving from California to Cincinnati. They expected me to arrive a week before Thanksgiving on an American Airlines flight, as usual. I didn't tell them I planned to move into The Buffalo Inn indefinitely. I didn't want to spoil the surprise of driving up in my new car with my dogs and a plan to stay for a while.

A road trip is something that can't be done on Maui unless a person circumnavigates the entire island several times, but then it wouldn't be a *real* road trip. I looked at an atlas of the mainland and decided to head for Moab. That's where Mitch's life as he knew it changed forever. I made a reservation at Sorrel River Ranch Resort, but didn't know how long I would stay. That's what a road trip is all about, keeping the plan open.

After two days of resting and massage at Sorrel, I took an easy five-hour float down the Colorado River. I was the only client; it was the last trip of the season, and I had to pay for three people because that was the minimum they took, but I didn't mind. There were very few tourists around the town, and some of the restaurants and activity places in Moab were already closed. It was during the float, where the female guide pointed out various rock formations and we talked about the names given them. In the near distance, there was a tall rock formation that looked like a hooded, robed priest. The formation was called The Protector, and it appeared like it was watching over the various formations beneath it. At that instant, I had my new idea, a perfect idea: I would write a book and call it *The Trust Protector*. That way I could turn this business of being a trust protector into a game, and deflect the hate coming at me from Carlotta Stone.

I know how to write a book. I wrote the history of a hospital, several family histories, and two lightweight mysteries set in Little Rock. I call them "airplane books." You get on flight on one coast and will be finished reading it by the time you reached the opposite side of the country. Writing the books helped me get over Harvey's sudden death and learn to live alone.

When the rafting company dropped me back at the ranch, I picked up my dogs from the resort's dog sitter, and we headed to the bookstore in Moab to buy a couple of blank journals and an ink pen, then to the local brewery for some craft beer, and on to the new Mexican restaurant, then back to the ranch for a hot-rock massage, and then I would pick up my new ink pen and begin. I stayed a little longer at Sorrel Ranch that I thought I would. I got on a roll with the story and didn't want to interrupt the muse. I'm in the editing stage right now, waiting for more ideas to come bubbling up.

Because I don't have a landline, all my calls with my daughters are on a cell, and they had no idea I hadn't been in Hawaii for the past month and Birdie calls me every morning.

A couple of hours before I was to arrive in Cincinnati, I texted Birdie that I missed my connection in Dallas and would be a couple of hours late. Then I drove to her house. She was in the yard decorating it for the holidays when I pulled up in my new car and rolled down the window. I think it took her a whole minute to recognize me. It was when the dogs started barking that she came out of her trance.

I got settled in The Buffalo Inn and joined an upscale sports club with a saline lap pool. Swimming is another thing that keeps me sane. I told Birdie about my trip cross-country, the book I was writing, and the trip I'd made to Little Rock to ambush Parsons. I described our encounter, and she wanted to know why I didn't just let things flow. Birdie has a unicorn-shitting-rainbows view on life, and she thought I could have created bad Karma by messing with Parsons.

I'd learned through all the years of being stalked by process servers and going to court to make conflict a game. That's why I went after that server in Maui. I wanted to fuck with him, The server that came up my stairs at night pushed a hot button in my psyche when he'd called out while banging at the door that he was "delivering a package for UPS that needed a signature." He'd scared me.

Birdie has an annual all women's party in December where her women friends get together, bring homemade cookies, drink, eat, and burn their grievances in a fire pit. I put Carlotta and the Beck sisters in the fire. This year, their party occurred on the last full moon of the decade. There must have been fifty women at her house, including a psychiatrist who brought her special stones and read the future with them, something she couldn't do in her medical office. I picked up one of the stones and she looked at it and said, "You are in a creative and turbulent period right now." I was impressed.

Birdie and I decided to drive down to Little Rock in my new Jeep Grand Cherokee for the no-contest clause hearing. We made it in ten easy hours. We hardly ran into any traffic. I reserved a room at a Residence Inn in North Little Rock. I didn't want to be anywhere near the Broadview compound.

On the drive down, Lee Edwards called me about a situation at Mitch's house that could become serious. The owner of Mr Handyman, Inc. one of his local informants, sent a carpenter to Carlotta's house to estimate a job and found a serious gas leak in the basement area. The workman reported the occupants weren't safe and neither were the neighboring homes. He informed the owner but she refused to fix the problem and so the company decided not to do the carpenter work.

We did a little bit of catching up, I liked Lee. He told me he'd bought a new helicopter, one like Mitch was going to get until he got sick, and every time he flew it, he thought of him. I wondered if some of the cash Mitch put in his pocket went toward his new toy. I hoped it did. Before the stroke that took out Mitch's ability to communicate efficiently, he filled me in on his relationship with Brass and with Lee. He figured one day the three of us would find ourselves in a situation together. Mitch said he'd taken care of both of them and he'd asked them to "keep an eye on my kids and my mom."

Birdie and I brainstormed about how to draw attention to the leak and I had a brilliant idea. I remembered the neighbor, Rob Riley, who had the fight with Carlotta over Piper toilet papering his house. I decided to make an appointment with him. I called his office but he wasn't available until the day of the hearing, and the only time he could see me was that morning. I took it—this couldn't wait.

I thought about the things Mitch had said about Riley—he'd been a prosecutor, he and Carlotta were enemies, he loved guns, and was big in a fundamentalist church. I told Birdie about the meeting with him and she wanted to come along, but I thought that might make it appear we were ganging up on him. I wanted her to go to the hearing with Doyle and give me the scoop on what happened.

Rob Riley didn't come to the reception area to greet me, and no one offered me sparkling water. I was shown into his office by his assistant and introduced to him. We sat across from each other at a small table; maybe it was an interrogation table. He was tall, well built, looked like he could play an Irish gangster in the movies. I knew I was dealing with a man who could smell bullshit a mile off.

I got to the point. "I'm Mitchell Stone's mother. I have evidence that his Broadview house is unsafe for his children to live in, and for the neighbors; it could explode or catch on fire at any time from a gas leak. Carlotta has known about it for over two weeks and has done nothing about it. I want someone from the neighborhood to call 9-1-1 and report smelling gas. It can't be me due to my history with her."

Riley locked eyes with mine. "Why did you choose me?"

"I know about your history with Carlotta; my son told me after the toilet papering incident. I read the police report. Mitch told me that you aren't a man to cross and aren't afraid of anyone."

"Do you have proof?" I gave him the handyman's report that Lee gave me. Riley also wanted to know who I'd told I was coming to see him. I said my daughter Birdie, but she'd keep it to herself.

He asked me what I thought was going to happen if he called, and I said, "The fire department will come and shut off the gas, notify the gas company. The cops or someone official will get involved and prevent anyone from going in there until the problem is fixed since the neighbors are at risk too. I think Carlotta will blow her top and probably accuse me of setting her up. I want to protect my grandchildren."

It wasn't a question but more a statement when he said, "You want something else to come out of this, don't you?"

I wasn't surprised. As a former prosecutor, Riley was in the business of looking for motives. "I want social services involved. I want pressure put on Carlotta to get help, and if she doesn't, then I want a judge to appoint a guardian for the kids. I don't want them in foster care. I think her sister would step up if things went that far, and I hope they don't. I'd move to Little Rock if that's what it took. My grandkids are in danger and I don't know how to help them."

Riley seemed to be careful with his words. "As an attorney, I can't help you. You don't have a relationship with your grandchildren, you don't even live in Arkansas, so you have no grandparent's rights, and I don't practice family law. As a neighbor, I appreciate the warning. Knowingly putting anyone's life at risk is a serious matter. If the house were to catch fire or explode and someone died or was injured, Carlotta Stone would be responsible."

Riley stood up, and I felt like I'd been dismissed. I thanked him for his time and asked him what I owed him, and he said, "Nothing but I understand you're worried and where the worry is coming from. I think this matter will probably resolve itself."

I felt like he was saying without words, *I've got this*. I wondered how long it would be before he picked up the phone and Carlotta's new shit show would start.

I walked down to the courthouse a few blocks away. Birdie had texted that the hearing was still going on. I waited outside by the door. I thought it was the same waiting area where I'd encountered the smelly process server.

Mitch came to my mind. I don't think he would have liked that I involved Riley. But it was the only way I could think to help for Piper and Milo. My intentions were good. But as the song title goes, "The Road to Hell Is Paved with Good Intentions."

I started thinking about who if anyone could reason with Carlotta about anything. It wasn't her sister or mother; maybe her personal assistant-babysitter,

Betty? I scrolled through my phone, checking for her number. I found it, but then I remembered I'd tried to call her several times over the years to check on how the children were doing and she wouldn't take my calls. Birdie and her sister Ginny had also tried and gotten nothing.

I hoped Riley went home, smelled gas, called 9-1-1. Would social services be called? I hoped so. I'd opened a Pandora's box. Maybe I should confront Carlotta when she walked out of the hearing, let everyone know about the dangerous house, and then she would feel pressure to fix it. But that would also cause more hate and she would do nothing. A neighbor was the way to go.

I waited for about thirty minutes before the door to the hearing room opened. I didn't recognize most of the people filing out but thought a couple of men looked like they might be reporters, then Carlotta's mother and sister walked past me, then Birdie and Doyle, Kelpe and his attorney, and finally Carlotta and her team of six along with a big man, tall and meaty, who looked to me like a bodyguard. He stayed close by her side and they left with Swainey and JoAnne.

Carlotta's entourage wore their poker faces but she was not. She picked up her step and walked past everyone like she'd just won the crown in a beauty contest. She wore her Barbie-goes-to-court-outfit. I thought it must have gone really bad for Kelpe. I didn't think Judge Graham would decide today, but the lawyers would have a sense of how it could go by the way the judge handled things.

Doyle saw me and put his index finger up to his lips and nodded his head for me to walk with him and Birdie back to his office. We didn't speak until we got there.

I was surprised when Doyle said, "That went well for Kelpe. He kept to the points, no drama, just the kind of presentation Judge Graham likes. If Carlotta's team prepared her, it didn't work. She was off the charts."

I wanted to hear all about that, but Doyle wanted to know why I wasn't present. I said I thought it would be better if I stayed away. Besides, this way I got the high points and not the boring stuff. I was glad he didn't ask me more, but figured he knew it was better to leave it alone.

Doyle said the judge asked Carlotta why she thought she had not violated the no-contest clause. "I know what your attorneys think but I want to hear your reasoning, Mrs Stone." Carlotta immediately went on a diatribe about how you murdered Mitch, and how you ganged up with Kelpe to control her inheritance. Judge Graham stopped her in mid rant. Carlotta said in a low voice, like what she had to say was just between the two of them, "You shouldn't be hearing my case because you know Elle Hawk. You understand what I'm talking about, don't you?" Graham told her she was excused.

Birdie thought the scene inside the court looked and sounded like a soap opera. Carlotta acted like she'd gotten the best of the judge. She sat down and stared at him, twisting her hair like she does, with this little smirk on her face. It was totally insane.The big guy guarding her looked like a B movie version of a bodyguard. His suit was too small, and he had on two different color socks.

The judge got out his dictionary and read the meaning of the word 'any' and 'contest' to Carlotta and her lawyers. He said keeping a dictionary handy helped attorney's and their clients understand simple words such as these. He explained how Carlotta's filing of lawsuits were by definition a contest to the trusts, even though she claimed her intentions were good and the fillings weren't contesting the trust. The judge asked her lawyers some questions and they beat around the bush and didn't answer and that seemed to irritate him, so he answered the questions for them. Carlotta sat there and puffed out her cheeks like a bored, spoiled kid. I think it finally dawned on her that she was going to lose. She grabbed Parsons by the lapels of his coat and said, "You said this wouldn't happen to me."

When Judge Graham left the hearing room, Birdie heard Carlotta say to her attorney, "Thanks for nothing. I had to take care of him myself." Her other attorneys looked at each other like WTF. Then she said, "Don't send me a bill for today. I had to do your work for you." Birdie said she wondered what kind of mood-altering drug Carlotta was taking to think she'd taken care of the Honorable Judge Graham.

Birdie and I walked down to a Thai restaurant and had just placed our order when she got a text. "It's Vivian, my friend who lives by Carlotta. I'm calling her back." Ten minutes later, she finished the call and filled me in on the dramatic events.

There's a police car, and a fire truck at Carlotta's house, and an animal control van with her dogs inside. The maid is sitting in her car and a cop is talking to her. The firemen are wearing gas masks, so Vivian guessed it had something to do with a gas leak.

Rob Riley said he smelled gas when he was walking around the side of his house. The closer he got to Carlotta's, the stronger the smell, especially near the basement window and he called 9-1-1.

When the firemen came out of the house, Riley spoke with them. He came back and told all of those standing around that the level of gas in the enclosed area under the house measured dangerously high and that, combined with live exposed wires on the ground, it was an extremely serious situation. If Mitch's house exploded, it could have destroyed the neighbors houses close to it.

Vivian was talking to Riley when one of the guys who worked for Mr. Handyman came up to him. Apparently, Riley called him that morning about a sudden leak under his sink. This guy told Riley that a couple of weeks ago, he had been at the Stones' and he told the owner the house was dangerous. He'd written it out on his report. Riley asked him if he had a copy and he did in his truck.

After asking a bunch of questions, Riley told him he needed to tell the officer, but the man said he didn't like cops and didn't want to. Vivian said Riley sounded like a preacher. She tried to imitate Vivian's imitation of him talking to the repair man. ***This is the Lord's way of asking you to help protect the innocent children. You will be doing the Lord's work. This is about accountability!***

*Vivian guessed he used that angle because the Mr. Handyman logo has a cross on it and a sticker on the van door—**This is a Christian Business**. She'd seen a lot of those stickers on local businesses lately and, not being a Christian, was put off by them.*

Riley walked with him over to the cop, and the three of them talked a while, and then Riley went back to his house with the handyman. The neighbors started leaving, the maid drove away, and someone put what looked like an official looking notice on the front door. Then a utility truck from the gas company came, and a worker was going over the yard with a metal detector.

When I heard the report of the happenings at Mitch's house, it seemed to me Riley admirably performed his Christian duty to protect the innocent. Too bad Carlotta's sister and mother had not seen it as their job to safeguard Piper and Milo. If they had, the coming shit show might not have happened.

CHAPTER 19 — JOANNE

After court, Carlotta, mother, and I went to the Copper Kettle for Lunch. Her body guard came to, but he sat at the bar. Carlotta sat down, ordered a vodka with cranberry juice, tossed it back and went to the ladies room. Mom asked me how I thought it went, I decided to tell what I really thought instead of what she wanted to hear.

"When Judge Graham pulled out his dictionary, I knew Carlotta was doomed. I never thought she had a chance in the first place. Remember, I told her before she went down this road a couple of years ago, to follow the trust as written, but she wouldn't listen. After that, and as always, I did what I could to support her. Kelpe's case against her is strong. I was impressed with his arguments."

"Don't tell you sister that, Just let it be. I'm too tired to take the drama if you tell her you think she has lost. You could be wrong."

"Before Mitch died, when she took his computer and had everything on it copied, I studied the trust and other documents and recommended to Carlotta that she live with the rules of the trust; it was extremely generous, and she would never have to work, and have plenty of extra spending money, but you didn't back me up. You told her what she wanted to hear; *fight—that's what strong women do*."

"I don't want to hear it. Enough!"

"No, Mother, it's not enough. Mitch was right to put her in a spending cage. All Carlotta could think about was beating him. She found lawyers who said she could break the trust and get her money free and clear. If I didn't tell her what she wanted to hear, she didn't listen to me I. That is the way she is; she was that way with the Mitch's doctors. She refuses to hear the truth if she doesn't like it."

True to her nature, my mother changed the subject and acted like I hadn't said a word. I couldn't let it go. "Mother, Carlotta is out of touch with reality. But she's never really been in touch with it since Daddy died. He was everything to her, while I was your favorite. We did the beauty pageant thing, while Dad and Carlotta did the farm things. She would ride on the tractor and go fishing with him and the dogs and he called her Mackie. Then he was killed, and she seemed to stay thirteen years old forever."

"Stop! She's coming back to the table."

Carlotta was on a high after her performance at court and was talking to her body guard at the bar and another man. I was glad I was driving after she drank a second vodka with cranberry juice before she ordered lunch. She kept going over and over what she'd said to the judge and to her attorneys.

Carlotta is good at putting on a front; she is an

excellent actress, learned it from Mother. Once she even fooled me. I actually believed she was a superstar Realtor and she had finally found her niche. One year, she won an award for sales at her company's local office in the Heights. It wasn't citywide but still, she won. Then I learned all her clients were friends of Mother, or people she knew. She had never represented a client she didn't know. She met Mitch through a friend of hers who was looking for rental property to buy.

My mind wandered during lunch. I started thinking about Carlotta when she married the first time. It took a year, but she planned a wedding that was the biggest event that farm town had ever seen. The flowers were even flown in from Hawaii, but it lasted less than eighteen months. He was a lawyer, his dad a judge. Six months into the marriage, her husband surprised her when he'd decided to focus his practice helping minorities, she left him and said to Mother, "We won't get rich with him helping poor people."

Then Carlotta met her "wood chopper." That was my dad's term for a man who could figure out how to get things done and do it himself. My dad was that way, and so was Mitch Stone except he used his wood chopper skills to make a fortune in a short period time.

My sister wanted Mitch and figured out how to get him by playing the hardworking Realtor. He was a man who respected hard working people. She also sucked up to his two girls, acting like the cool older sister. All seemed happy the first six months, and I thought at age thirty she might start to grow up. The real her couldn't stay hidden and the selfish little girl came back out to stay.

One of Mother's friends came up to the table and that brought me out of my trip to the past. Carlotta gave another stellar performance about her "taking it to Judge Graham" and "doing my lawyers jobs for them." I had to put a stop to it and pointed to my watch and lied. "I have a conference call with a client. I need to get going."

Since Mitch died, I'd spent a lot of time in Little Rock helping Carlotta. She had hired help, but she needed guidance, and I tried to give it professionally and personally. When I saw Voodoo Yoga, it was proof she and her children were out of control,

When we pulled into the compound after our lunch, there was a truck from the utility company getting ready to leave. The driver said the gas and electricity to the house had been turned off by the fire department and they were checking the gas lines in the yard for leaks.

Carlotta became visibly upset, "There's not any leak inside the house. Get back in there and turn the gas back on. It's cold, and the furnace needs to work. Go do your job."

The driver put his truck in gear and got ready leave. He didn't look like the kind of man who would put up with that kind of talk from a woman. I rushed in to explain.

"Please, forgive my sister's rudeness. She has had a bad shock this morning. I just have one question if you don't mind, please."

"Ask it."

"How did the utility company find out about the leak inside of the house?"

"A neighbor smelled gas outside and called it in. The fire guys came, they found a high level of gas inside the place." He put the truck back in gear and pulled away as soon as he finished speaking.

I asked Carlotta if she'd gotten a call from one of the neighbors, or the maid, or the police, and she said her lawyer told her to turn off her cell before she went into the hearing and she forgot to turn it back on. She scrolled through and found a number of missed calls and texts. I couldn't believe she had forgotten to turn her best friend on. It was alway on and in her pocket, or her bra, or her hand.

"Let's go over to The Playhouse and sort it out," and I walked off. As we were walking up the steps to the house, a police car drove up and a well-dressed man got out and introduced himself as Bill Brass, LRPD detective. He showed us his ID and said he was following up on the officer's report on the emergency situation at the Stone property. A uniformed officer was with him but stayed in the police car when Brass came inside with us.

Carlotta stayed very quiet, which is what she does when she's unsure of herself. She wasn't the same person who told attorneys she'd done their job for them. I knew something was off. I wanted to take the lead but if I did Carlotta would resent it, so I held back. I couldn't figure out why a detective would be involved in the matter of a gas leak.

Detective Brass went through the fire department report and handed Carlotta a copy. He asked if she was aware there was a gas leak, and she said she wasn't. She said that she'd been out of town for a couple of weeks over the holidays and things were fine when she left. She had no idea there was a problem and was thankful it was found. My sister was being very polite. She even thanked him.

Brass handed Carlotta something that looked like job estimate and said a carpenter with Mr. Handyman repair service had done a work order on the house a few weeks ago. It described the work and the approximate cost. Across the bottom of the page was written in bold lettering, "Dangerous gas leak under the house. Recommended immediate shut off. Owner advised house unsafe and cannot not do work until the leak repaired."

I took both reports from Carlotta, looked over them and asked Brass where he got information from Mr.

Handyman and was told the carpenter provided it to the officer earlier today. "It's in the report, take a look."

"How did this carpenter just happen to be here today? Quite a coincidence, I think."

Brass gestured toward the paper. "He was doing work in the neighborhood, saw the emergency vehicles, wondered if the Stone house had caught fire, and came over out of curiosity, so it says if you will read it."

Carlotta interrupted me before I could ask another question "I think someone is trying to set me up— probably Elle Hawk That's something she would do. I never called a handyman."

"Who is Elle Hawk?"

"She is my husband's mother and wants to get me removed from his trust. I just got out of court today about it. Hawk murdered him and his attorney WP Kelpe helped her get away with it and now they are after my money." Carlotta went on and on with her usual rant about Hawk and Kelpe. Brass let her talk and get it all off her chest. I was impressed with his patience, but also suspicious. It wasn't relevant to the issue.

"I'm my sister's attorney. I would like to better understand why the police are involved in this matter. No crime has been committed. It is a simple gas leak." I was hoping Carlotta would keep quiet but I could see her revving up for another rant.

Brass handed me another report, this one describing the scene underneath the house and in the bedrooms: rat's and raccoon's nests, chewed electrical wires through out the basement area, leaking gas lines. He had pictures showing these things. My sister grabbed them out of my hand.

Carlotta said, "That looks like something someone did when I was out of town—set up a scene like that to hurt or kill me or make me look bad. Whoever did it probably called Mr. Handyman and pretended she was me. This is a setup. Elle Hawk did this!"

The detective explained, "Ma'am the fire department's report indicates that based on the age of the nests, the animal tracks in the dirt, and so on, the situation under the house has been going on for a long time. The report cited extreme hoarding of stacked-up papers, clothing, and other flammable materials tightly packed in the lower part of the house that would act as kindling if a fire were to start. Fire is great concern, but an explosion would be a disaster. If the wires were to spark inside an area filled with gas, it would detonate and probably take the house we were sitting in with it and damage other homes close to the explosion."

I was shocked when I heard all this. I hadn't been in Carlotta's downstairs in, well, I don't remember, probably before Mitch died. The Playhouse showed signs of the same things in the rooms that mother and I didn't use, but I ignored that since I usually didn't go in them.

Carlotta said in a cocky voice, "It looks to me like your job is to find out who has put me and my children in danger. Isn't that why you're telling me this?"

She was doing what she did best— play the victim. I wanted to hear what Brass had to say and how he would say it considering her tone and the way she rolled her eyes.

I was impressed with his patience. "Mrs. Stone, the people who investigate how any fire starts are the same ones who came in here and inspected your house. There is no indication in the report that this is a setup. The problem has been going on for a while. You claim you didn't know about gas leaks, but the document indicates otherwise."

"Someone could have done this a while back, for all you and the experts know. I don't go under the house."

I wished my sister would keep quiet.

"The officer spoke with your maid, and she said before you left on vacation, a carpenter came to the house. She remembers that because you told her not to clean the den in the downstairs area until he was gone, and that made her late for her next cleaning job."

"That is a lie. She can't speak English. She's Mexican; I only hire them because they don't speak any English. I have to point at the things I want done."

Brass took out a cell phone and showed Carlotta a picture of a middle-aged, dark brown-haired, short woman, wearing a blue shirt and black pants. She wore a name tag that indicated she worked for a maid service. "Do you recognize this woman?" and Carlotta yes. It was the maid, Brass played a video as she spoke to the officer using fluent but heavily accented English.

"The problem you face here, Ma'am, is you were told your house was dangerous, you allowed a maid to come while you were away to feed your dogs and work here. You returned to this house with your minor children, but you have done nothing to remedy a dangerous situation that put your family, your neighbors, and the maid at risk."

Carlotta started to speak but stopped herself as. I stepped in and asked Brass if he was accusing my sister of committing a crime.

"I'm following up on the officer's report. Social services has been contacted because the safety of minor children is involved." He unclipped a business card from his file and handed it to Carlotta. "You need to contact this case worker within twenty-four hours to schedule an appointment for an evaluation of your children's living situation if they are going to stay here while your house is repaired."

Carlotta dropped the card on the floor in front of him and left the room. Mother followed her. A few minutes later, Mother came back and said it was time to pick up the children from school and she was going with Carlotta to get them. I was glad for them to leave the house. That stunt, dropping the card in front of Brass and walking off, was typical thirteen-year-old Carlotta behavior.

Brass said he would accompany me to the house to get what Carlotta and the children would need until it was safe to return. I said that wasn't necessary because it wasn't dangerous any longer. He said that wasn't the point. "I'm taking Ms Stone's concern someone has created this dangerous situation to harm her seriously. That makes her house a potential crime scene that can't be disturbed until we thoroughly investigate. Soon as you get what she needs, I'll have a guard posted."

I walked over to the house with Brass. I told him this whole thing felt off. More was going on that he was letting on. I had mixed feelings about him but couldn't figure why.

"I know trouble when I see it, and your sister and her children are in trouble. They need help. I'm up-to-date on her background, the reports concerning her minor children in the past and currently. If someone doesn't get this widow and her kids help, I'm afraid of what will happen to them. This, what happened today, is a wake-up call."

"You don't believe that story about a setup, do you? I think you're sealing off this place so Carlotta can't get back into the house but I don't know why. Most of all I am wondering why you are here."

He didn't comment right away. "Mitch Stone did a lot of good in this town, things he didn't brag about but the city appreciated. Someone needs to look out for his kids. It's obvious their mother isn't up to it, so we're going to do it for Mitch."

I asked him, "Who are the *we* you are referring to?"

"People who care."

CHAPTER 20 — BILL BRASS

I left the Stone Compound and the officer drove us back to the station. I filled Marshall in on what was going on. As a long time friend of the Stone and Walker men, this problem with Carlotta Stone was personal for him. I folded my six-foot-four frame into my silver Porsche and pulled out of the station lot, and headed for my home on Wye Mountain.

When I moved from Denver, all I knew about the South was from the movie *Deliverance.* One of the first things I noticed about Little Rock and figured it was probably typical down here was the web of relationships between people who have lived here for generations. “Incestuous” is the word that came to mind.

Mitch Stone and his father, and Max Walker and his father, were in the highway and road construction business. Marshall Knight, grew up in the Hillcrest area of Little Rock and was good friends with Izzy and Elle. After the sisters married Walker and Stone, Knight became friends with their husbands.

Mitch and Max, and their fathers, all died from cancer due to long-term exposure to chemicals in asphalt and other petroleum-based products. Max’s dad died first, from kidney cancer, and then Mitch’s of the same thing two years later. Then Max was diagnosed with bladder cancer and died. Not long his death, Mitch met the same fate.

One friend after another dying so close together devastated Marshall Knight. He promised Mitch he would make sure his kids be watched over. That's the reason he asked me to look into the Carlotta Stone matter when the gas leak incident came up.

It was a good move for me, migrating to Little Rock, going to work for the LRPD as a detective. Marshall Knight was an old friend and now I'm his go-to man for things he wants done outside of normal police work.

I was about to make my turn to head up the mountain when I got a call from the officer I'd placed at the Stone house. He'd heard a commotion inside and found the boy, Milo, inside screaming. He'd crawled in through a window in one of the downstairs bedrooms and a raccoon bit him.

The officer then bagged the raccoon alive, and animal control came and took it for a rabies test. He called 9-1-1 after Milo passed out and tumbled down the steps. Carlotta Stone couldn't be located. I asked him what hospital, called Marshall, and turned around and headed back to town.

Social services becomes involved in cases of domestic abuse or child neglect and they make sure children are living in a safe, stable environment. The Stone situation was neither safe nor stable. When I arrived, I informed the nurse at reception of the situation and asked that she contact the proper agency.

I asked the ER physician how Milo was doing and if I could see him and maybe ease his mind about what was going on. While I was speaking with her, Marshall Knight walked in with Elle Hawk. I hadn't seen her since we met at the Marriott. A woman who looked like she could be Mitch's sister was with them.

I didn't realize how close Marshall and Elle were until I saw them together looking like old friends, picking up as if no time had passed since they were last together. She touched his arm, "I think you and Brass should go in first, make Milo feel safe, let him know you knew his dad and grandad, and then bring me and Birdie in. It's been three years, and you know what he's been told." The chief agreed, and the physician attending Milo took us back to the exam room.

Milo Stone was sitting up in bed with an IV drip in his arm, a bandage on his forearm, closure strips over his right eyebrow, and an aide sitting in a chair next to his bed. I thought the boy looked small for a kid almost thirteen, but I didn't know anything about kids. When I was that age, I could easily pass for fifteen. Milo's medium cut blond hair curled around his face, his eyes were a cold blue, he looked smart, and when he spoke I knew he was. He had the coloring of his parents.

Milo didn't wait for introductions. He said, "I know you." He was looking at Marshall. "You spoke at the dedication for the new entrance to the park that was in honor of my dad. You're the chief of police."

Marshall smiled, "You're right. And this is Detective Bill Brass. We both knew your dad, granddad, and uncles. We're here to make sure you're OK, because I know your dad would want us to do that."

"I'm worried the raccoon that bit me has rabies. I've seen raccoons around, but I've never seen one that looked sort of drunk— that's a symptom. The one with the babies wasn't the one that did it."

"We will find that out soon. The animal is being tested and we will know in twelve hours. Milo why did you climb through a window to get into the house? Why not ask the officer to go inside with you."

"I needed my laptop, and my mom said the cop guarding the door would never let me go in. She said the police were harassing us."

"I've been trying to contact your mom to let her know you are here. Have any suggestions where I might find her?"

"I stay by myself a lot, so it's nothing to worry about, Mom not being home."

"What about Piper—where is she?"

"Mom and JoAnne and Swainey were having a big fight and Piper left. She's probably down the street at her best friend's or with her new boyfriend. Who knows? I want to go home now."

Marshall explained, "The doctor wants to keep you overnight for observation. Who would you like for me to call and let know you are here? Maybe Piper could spend the night with you. Does she have a cell?"

"Mom's missing so there is just my Aunt JoAnne and Swainey, she's Mom's mother."

Marshall said he would make sure they knew. "I called your grandmother, Elle. She's a friend of mine. I know you haven't seen her since your dad died, but she's here with your Aunt Birdie, and they'd like to see you, if that's okay."

"Mom won't let me and Piper see them."

Marshall asked, "But would you like to?"

Milo didn't hesitate, "Yes,"

Marshall patted Milo on the shoulder, left the room, and came back in with Elle Hawk and Birdie. If anything good came out of the raccoon bite, this was it. We stayed a while before we left the three of them huddled up together jabbering.

Marshall and I walked out of the emergency entrance when a Cadillac sports car screeched to a stop in front of the entrance. Carlotta Stone jumped out and ran inside screaming for Milo. She didn't put the car in gear and it rolled backward and hit a post, blocking the drive.

She banged on the double doors, trying to get into the area that can only be opened by the staff. Hospital security came, a nurse tried to reason with her —Carlotta slapped the nurse across the face. The security guard took her out of the waiting room. It wasn't long before a police car arrived and hauled Carlotta down to the station. Carlotta Stone was in our territory now.

CHAPTER 21 — ELLE HAWK

I was reeling from the excitement of the long day—the hearing, the gas leak, the police at the house, the raccoon bite, Milo in the hospital, Carlotta's melt down, and the best of all was our victory for Mitch's no-contest clause.

Everyone thought Judge Graham wouldn't rule for a couple of weeks, but we were wrong. By three that afternoon, his order was posted on the Pulaski Clerk website. Carlotta Stone lost. That probably contributed to her performance at the hospital.

Milo was happy to see me and Birdie. I felt it in our long hug and how his tense little body relaxed as I held him. I tried not to cry but tears came. For the first time since Mitch died, I had hope that my grandchildren would have a chance for some kind of healthy life, and that included a relationship with me, Birdie, Ginny, and Mitch's aunts, uncles and cousins.

Birdie and I sat on the bed with Milo, she with her hands on his feet like she had with Mitch when he was in the hospital, and I held his hand. Milo asked a lot of questions about what I thought was going to happen to him and Piper. The questions surprised me. I didn't think kids his age thought about things like social services and how it applied to them, especially ones that took private jets to Aspen, and lived in upscale neighborhoods, and went to high-end private schools, and had plenty to eat even though it was takeout.

Milo was an articulate kid. “I’m worried Piper and I might have to go live with Swainey or Aunt JoAnne if something happens to Mom. A social worker will come to the house and see the mess in Shelly’s old room. It's full of hoarding. Mom keeps the door shut so no one will see it. The maid isn't allowed in there either. I found a little hole where the rats and raccoons are getting in. Mom keeps saying she would get it fixed.” Birdie asked Milo how long the room had been in that condition.

“Mom never threw anything away, but she kept it neat. After Dad died, it got a whole lot worse. Piper and I watched these shows about hoarding, I like them just as much as *Doctor Pimple Popper*, and I know it is a sickness. Rich people hoard not just poor ones who live in slums. I think it is like a drug habit.”

Milo changed the subject. “Mom had a tree with dolls hanging on it. That’s supposed to be a secret too but I found it and she took it down. You can see it on YouTube.” Birdie told him she had discovered the tree room when his dad was in hospital. They talked about the tree for a while.

Milo got on the subject of rabies testing in animals, the symptoms in humans, and that the treatment was a series of shots that were painful. We just let him run with it until he ran out of steam and got sleepy. He was moved into a room, and we stayed the night with him. It surprised me that neither JoAnne or Swainey had stopped by the hospital to see him. I wondered why.

I was angry that Carlotta had let her house go downhill to the degree it was infested with rats and raccoons and her mother and sister had done nothing about it. I called Doyle and told him what was going on and asked what I could do legally, and he said, "Nothing."

I thought about driving out to Mitch's house and getting some clothes for Milo but I didn't want to run into JoAnne or her mother. I thought about calling Marshall and asking if he'd found out anything about Carlotta but thought it was better to let it alone. I called WP, filled him in, and asked him if he had any clothes that would fit Milo, warm up pants, sweat shirt, socks, something he could wear instead of a hospital gown. Within an hour he arrived bringing some of his youngest sons sweat pants and tops he had outgrown.

It was close to noon before Milo woke up. Birdie was sitting near the foot of his bed with her feet on the mattress. She had gone to Izzy's earlier and taken a shower and changed into clean clothes and then I did the same and brought back Shipley donuts, cinnamon buns, hot chocolate, egg biscuits, fruit juices.

When I saw his eyes open, I put my hand on his forehead and it felt a little too warm. "Hey, how are you feeling?"

Milo tucked his nose into the neck of the gown,

"I stink and I've got a bad taste in my mouth."

"Well, hanging on the back of the bathroom door is a set of clean clothes. There's shampoo and toothpaste and a toothbrush in the shower area. Need help getting out of bed?"

I didn't want to hover over him but I wanted him to feel safe.

Milo sat up and hung his legs over the side of the bed, picked up the remote, lowered the bed, and stood up, grabbed the back of the open gown and walked into the bathroom. We heard the shower start and he was in there a long time. When he came out, his hair was brushed, and the clothes actually fit him.

Birdie had set out the donuts, rolls, egg biscuits, hot chocolate, and orange juice. Milo sat on the edge of the bed, put the tray in his lap and began to devour everything on his plate.

The door opened and a young woman walked in. "Hello Milo, I'm Judy Evans. I think you might be looking for this." She sat the laptop on his bed.

The look on Milo's face when he picked it up and hugged it to his chest was total joy. "How did you get it?"

Evans smiled, "You must be a big shot around here. The chief of police himself asked me to drop it by."

"He knew my dad," Milo said as he flipped the top up.

"I'm Milo's grandmother, Elle Hawk. You just made Milo a happy guy. Thank you."

"I was coming by this morning anyway. I'm from social services, just stoping by checking on Milo and introducing myself." She handed him her card and gave one to me.

"I know all about social services," Milo said, looking up at her and she said, "Then I bet you know why I came by."

"The raccoon bite, mess at the house, gas leak, the missing mom," Milo didn't look up. He was looking up something on his computer screen.

Judy Evans wore her medium-length, dark-brown hair pulled back from her face and tucked behind her ears. Her body showed the hours she spent working out. She looked to be in her early thirties and wore tight jeans, a white sweater under an expensive-looking leather jacket, and a pair of brown leather riding boots. I wondered if she usually dressed this way for her work.

Milo turned the screen toward Judy—"My latest creation, *Voodoo Yoga in the Heights*. My friend Clifton and I made it. The next morning we learned it went viral overnight. I want to write scripts and make videos."

"That was yours. I've seen it. I'm impressed. How did you know about that Voodoo Yoga place?"

He grinned, "That's a secret. You want to hear about the raccoon?" She did and Milo was happy to tell the story of his break in and the attack.

It was fun for me watching their interaction, his laughter and easy manner with her, and then it suddenly ended.

CHAPTER 22 — MILO STONE

I sleep on my right side with my open palm between the pillow and my face, my legs are bent and my back a little rounded. I start on my back but wake up in this position. I dream a lot and hardly every wake up during the night. I opened my eyes and felt my eye lashes brush against my palm and saw Birdie sitting at the side of my bed near the foot. She wore red socks with tiny yellow kittens on them and a T shirt with a rainbow unicorn on the front, but her jeans were normal. She was reading a hard cover book—not a Kindle.

Gran walked out of the bathroom door and she was dressed sort of like Dad used to in the winter—corduroy jeans with a flannel long sleeve button up shirt and a Patagonia vest and flat brown suede boots.

I didn't say anything just looked at them and thought about the raccoon bite and why I was here. Until last night, I never thought I would ever see Gran or Birdie again. Gran came up to the bed and asked how I was feeling. I told her I smelled bad and she told me to take a shower and I did. I stood under the hot water a long time and let it beat the top of my head and back. My eyebrow didn't really hurt but the bite felt hot and it throbbed. I couldn't quit thinking rabies.

Grand and Birdie and I ate a great breakfast together and then the best thing happened, a social worker came in and brought me my computer. Her name was Judy and she was really cool and we talked about lots of fun stuff and then it ended. Swainey and JoAnne came in and tried to run Gran and Aunt Birdie off, but they didn't move and neither did Judy.

Swainey and JoAnne are opposites of Gran and Birdie in every way but especially in the way they dressed. Swainey had gray hair but she dyed it blond and it was fixed in place with spray or gel or something. She aways wore pant suits and shoes with low heels. When she was at the lake she still wore the same thing. I'd never seen her in shorts or skirts or a dress. My aunt dyes her hair brown and that is her natural color. I guess it was getting gray and she thought this would hide it. She always wears V neck tops, with her skirts, or shorts, or jeans. Says the V is her signature. Today she was wearing all black and Swainey was in a pink suit.

When Aunt JoAnn ordered Gran out, I thought to myself—what would Dad do?

"Shut up!" I stood up a little too fast—the tray tipped over and the food hit the floor and the hot chocolate landed in front of Swainey and bounced up her pants' leg. She jumped back and screamed.

Swainey turned toward Gran and said, "You are a bad influence on Milo."

I'm smart, my IQ is 143, my teachers notice but not Swainey or JoAnne, Dad did, and Mom was always saying I was too smart for my own good. I wanted them to know that I knew things.

"I don't want you all to keep on being mean to Gran. I know the truth—she didn't murder Dad. Piper knows the truth too. I know another big thing, and I bet you all don't. I'm adopted." I didn't plan to say that part —it just came out.

Aunt JoAnne made a little smirk and rolled her eyes like I was making up a story. "Really, don't be foolish enough to think we are going to believe that."

I had to defend myself. I looked at Judy Evans and wondered if I should shut up but I couldn't. "I found out when I was going through Mom's desk. She went to a clinic in California. She paid them to make an embryo and she adopted it and they implanted it into her body."

Swainey interrupted, "Honey, that is science fiction."

"I read all about it on the internet after I saw the report from the clinic. I scanned the paperwork into my computer so I could prove I knew the truth. I will show you," and reached for my computer

"Milo, that's not true," Swainey said. "You're a McSwain."

"No! Right after Dad died I went to his Twenty-Three and Me account and found out that Piper was related to Gran and Aunt Birdie, but I wasn't. I thought it must be wrong, but I couldn't get it out of my mind, and then I found the adoption papers. Just like I found Dad's medical reports and his trusts and lots of other things. I'm good at research."

Gran came to the bed and took my hand. "Milo, please don't think your dad loved you any less than he loved Piper because you aren't genetically related."

"You're just trying to make me feel better about it."

"Shut up Elle. All this is your fault. You put these ideas in his mind. Now get out of here before I call security." Aunt JoAnne sounded really angry.

Gran ignored her and put her hand on my shoulder. "Your dad found out about this when you were five and we talked about it several times. He didn't like being lied to by your mother, but he didn't hold it against you. He was proud of how intelligent you are and how good you are at riding dirt bikes. He said you were fearless and he liked that. Even after he found out, your dad talked about how you were like him in a lot of ways. You are a clean freak like he was. He took at least two showers a day. He used to say, 'Shower at night to clean off the day and take one in the morning to start the new day.' He also showered after a work out at the gym or riding and other times he felt dirty—same as you."

I don't think I've ever had Swainey's or Aunt JoAnne's complete attention until now. I told them, "I know why the social worker is here. One reason is no one could find Mom, but the main one is because me and Piper have been living in a house that could have blown up. Now, I've probably been exposed to rabies because no one made her get rid of all that junk that has raccoons living in it." I found myself getting a little mad because they should have helped Mom and us. I waited for them to say something, especially Aunt JoAnne, because she's a lawyer, but she didn't. So I said the rest of what was on my mind. "Piper and I know Mom is sick and she's a prescription drug addict; you all do too, but you haven't helped her. You enabled her. I know how things work."

Aunt JoAnne stood up, "That is enough! You've said ridiculous and hurtful things." She looked at Judy Evans, "It's time for you to leave. Milo needs rest."

Judy said, "That's not up to you Ma'am."

Swainey pointed her finger at Gran and raised her voice, practically a screech, "That woman put lies in his head. She's always been a trouble maker."

I raised my voice but I didn't yell. "I'm not a liar. I have proof! If I wanted to, I could spend my time watching porn on the internet like some of my friends, I'm alone most of the time when I'm home and that gives me plenty of time to go through Mom's stuff and other things in the house, and I learn things from the internet. In case you don't know it Swainey, I have the IQ of a genius. So quit acting like I am stupid."

Swainey started to cry, but I didn't feel sorry for her. JoAnne stood up and looked at Gran and said, "You did this. Stay away from our family." She sounded just like my mother, and I was glad that I wasn't genetically related to any of the McSwains.

Gran said, "Honey, try not to worry. I have some really smart people helping me and we're going to figure out a way to help you and your mom and Piper. I hope Swainey and JoAnne will help too." Gran looked at them. Aunt JoAnne and Swainey just looked back at Gran and said nothing.

Then Swainey said to me, "I will bring Piper to see you this afternoon," and they walked out the door.

"That was intense," was all Gran said.

Judy Evans came over to the bed and touched my hand, "Get some rest. You've got my card, call me if you need something. I'll be back tomorrow." She gave my hand a little squeeze. "I forgot," she pulled my cell out of her back pocket and handed it to me.

Aunt Birdie said, "If it's okay with you Milo, I'm going to call your dad's uncles and aunts, get all the cousins tougher, and tell them to stop by. I know everyone misses you.I know you must miss the farm, the Christmas parties, and fishing with yours cousins."

The doctor came in and said the raccoon tested positive for rabies and he was going to start the treatments. He wanted me to spend another night in case I had an adverse reaction. The first shot really hurt. The needle went in right next to the bite. I'd read that's the way it was done, but it burned like fire. Then the doctor told me to close my eyes and rest.

I must have gone to sleep. When I opened my eyes, Piper was in the room. I was so glad to see her, I thought I would cry. She got in bed with me and we snuggled up like we used to do when we were little kids. Aunt Birdie left and said she'd come back and bring fried chicken and lemon pie for dinner. Gran was out at her sister Izzy's house and was making it for us.

Piper told me what had been happening at the house and with Mom and then she said, "I am not going to go to school for a while. Everyone knows about the stunt Mom pulled at the hospital. Someone in the waiting room recorded it on a cell and put it on YouTube."

Piper handed me her phone and I watched Mom acting like a totally crazy person. Who ever took it was good. They panned the crowded waiting area and got the reactions of the watchers. When Mom slapped the nurse, you could hear the whack. It was great.

"There was something on the local news about *How Safe Is Your Neighborhood*? It used our house as an example of how a gas leak in a neighbor's house could put other homes around it in danger." Piper looked upset and about to cry.

When Gran and Aunt Birdie came in with the dinner, the smell of the fried chicken reminded me of Clifton's mom the night we did the video. That seemed like a long time ago, so much had happened. I haven't talked to Clifton since. I call, but it always goes to his voice mail. I text, but he doesn't text back.

Gran said she had an idea she wanted to run by me and Piper. "Izzy said we could all stay out at her place until your house is fixed. She and a friend are going traveling together for a little while. Birdie and I are going to stay there and take care of her parrot while she's gone. You and Piper can stay with us if you want."

I hadn't seen Aunt Izzy since Dad died. She used to take us up and down the river on her speed boat all the time, and let us ride the horses. Her house is built way up off the ground and is close to the edge of the river. She has a couple of acres and two horses and a greenhouse and a full-time yard man there to take care of her gardens and waterfalls and koi pond.

The house is practically all glass, and there isn't a ceiling, just the inside of the roof, which is mostly skylights. She calls it her tree house. There aren't any permanent walls but partitions that she moves around to change things up. Aunt Izzy has a green parrot, the breed where the males are green and the females are red. It has a glassed-in aviary. But she lets it fly free in the house when she's home, and it goes up in the rafters. It's trained to poop in one spot. Really cool.

I liked Gran's idea about living with Auntie Birdie and Gran at Aunt Izzy's, and so did Piper.

I asked Gran, "What about Mom? Can she come too?" And that's when we found out that Mom was going to a treatment center for a while and I wouldn't get to see her before she left. Gran told us that the same kind of thing happened to her mom after her dad was killed, and her grandma came and lived with them.

I told Gran that Swainey or Aunt JoAnne would never let me and Piper stay with her. "Mom's will says if something happens to her, then Aunt JoAnne or Swainey will take us and our trust would pay two hundred thousand dollars a year until we were eighteen. They pretend to be rich, but they aren't, and that money would be a good reason for one of them to take us."

Gran said, "Your mom isn't dead, so maybe that doesn't apply but I will find out. I want you and Piper to think about what I said and decide what you want, and I'll make things work out until your mom gets well and comes home. If you decide to stay with Swainey or JoAnne, that's fine too. I want you and Piper to feel safe and happy. That's what your dad would want, and I think your mom would too."

Piper hadn't said anything since Gran started talking about staying at Aunt Izzy's and Gran asked her what she was thinking.

Piper said, "I don't want to go with Swainey to Lonoke or with Aunt JoAnne; we would be second best to her kids. I'd rather go with you and Aunt Birdie. And I don't want to see Mom for a while either. I'm mad at her."

Gran said, "Let me see what I can do."

Sometimes I see Dad in Gran's face and I wish I was genetically related to them, but I suppose it's enough Gran and Birdie love me.

CHAPTER 23 — ELLE HAWK

I left Birdie and Piper with Milo and was walking down the hall toward the elevator when I saw Bill Brass, long and lean dressed in pressed jeans and a long sleeved plaid shirt, standing by the nurses station. The young nurse was flirting with him. I might have done the same thing myself thirty years ago. Brass wanted to have a talk with me.

"Let's go over to the Big Orange. They have my favorite beer and we can do our talking there. I'm not much of a hospital person. Had enough of it with Mitch's ordeal." He said I reminded him a little of Izzy. He mentioned they'd had a few beers at the Orange once when her son was in hospice, just a couple of days before he died.

We drove over in his sports car, settled into a booth, and I found we both liked Duvel.

Brass asked me how I was holding up and I said, "I could walk away from all this drama and just let what happens happen. I don't have any rights as a grandmother, so I've been told, but I can't walk away. As to holding up, I have a lot of experience with crazy."

"I'm guessing you know that Carlotta has agreed to go into addiction treatment and therapy."

"I heard. I thought she would have been

arrested for hitting the nurse, but now she's going to a clinic. Sounds like a miracle."

"That's what I wanted to go over with you. No one wants Mitch's wife to go down the drain, and she's headed in that direction. That was a big hit she took, getting herself kicked out of the trust. Why did she go down that road?"

"Stubborn, narcissistic, greedy, all that, but the good thing is, the kids will always have whatever they need and she can't take it from them. Besides, she's not broke, though she'll never live close to the lifestyle she would have had if she had followed the grand plan, unless she finds another Mitch. Talk about comeuppance. So what happened—this treatment center business?"

"Her sister came down to the station a couple of hours after Carlotta was brought in, and we had a talk. I laid out the reasons why her sister was in a bad situation, although I'm sure she was aware of them—the kids' unsafe living conditions, driving under the influence of more than alcohol, the assault on the nurse, and a few other incidents she's been involved in since Mitch died."

"I *suggested* to JoAnne that if her sister entered a drug treatment program immediately, went into therapy with a licensed therapist, got counseling for the children, hired a full-time housekeeper, then her children wouldn't be removed from the home. She would be required to prove she and her children were attending therapy sessions and whatever else is required by social services. If these conditions were met, we felt sure the nurse would forget about the slap in the face—with a little compensation."

"What did JoAnne say to all of that?"

"She said she would think about it and talk to her mother. I pushed and said I needed her answer immediately, otherwise I couldn't say what would happen. She knew what I meant and said she would convince her sister this was the best way to go."

"I can't believe Carlotta will follow this new grand design for her life? She's famous for agreeing to something she doesn't intend to do. Plus, she didn't have sense enough to follow Mitch's plan for her life, in spite of the consequences, so why would she agree to this?"

"I think her sister will convince her."

"How can I get in on this? Birdie and I are willing to move down here, stay at my sister's, if the kids will be allowed to see us on a regular basis or, better yet, they can live with us until Carlotta is well. Swainey isn't capable. Look what she's let happen."

"Here's the name of an attorney who can help. He wrote the name on a napkin. "She'll explain the logistics. I've spoken with her about this."

"Thanks. On another Carlotta topic, I talked to the owner of the handyman service. He can have the house ready in two weeks—get rid of the pests, the hoarding, sanitize the place, fix the leaks, the whole thing. Going to be very pricey. I called WP and he approved the expenditure."

"Good to hear. Now, I'm going to order a burger and have another Duvel. What about you, Elle?"

"I'll have the garden burger and another beer. You know, I experienced some of what Milo and Piper are going through. I told Milo about it today, hoping it would make him feel better. After all, Izzy and I turned out just fine."

"What happened?"

"My dad died in a plane crash when I was six. My mother went crazy too, and took up with a man called Skeet. He was, according to one of my aunts, a real good-looking, sweet-talking thief. They stole a car, drove it over the state line, and got caught. My grandmother was advised to have Mother declared incompetent and committed to the state hospital so she wouldn't go to prison. She stayed over a year getting shock treatments. When she was released, my grandma lived with us, raised us, and Mother worked. I was sixteen when Grandma died and we felt lost. I imagine Milo and Piper feel the same way"

"Elle, there's a whole network of men that were close to Mitch and have been keeping an eye on his kids. They've been waiting for the chance to help them, do it for Mitch, because of what he'd done for them. I'm one of those guys, but I'm not going into why. Carlotta hasn't got a chance against us now it's out in the open. She has to comply or she'll lose them."

The server brought the food, and Brass and I sat in silence for a while, digesting the day along with the beer and burgers. Izzy had told me a little about him, how she didn't like him when they first met, when he was looking into a case and thought her son Max had something to do with it. Over time, she said they have become casual friends.

We were finishing up and waiting for a dessert we planned to share when I started telling Brass another story. "Not long ago I was driving across country and stayed in Taos for several days. I met a woman at a cafe who was having a book signing party. I picked up a copy and saw she was a psychic and her book was about crystal therapy. After the party broke up, we got to talking, and she said, when I came in the door, she saw a Golden Eyelash Viper hovering over my left shoulder. She nodded to the snake and it disappeared."

I went on, "I call Carlotta the Golden Eyelash Viper. Lee Edwards gave her that name. Anyway, the psychic asked my permission to do a reading. I took notes on a napkin, put it in a text, and sent it to myself." I scrolled down and found it and handed my cell to Brass.

A woman is sitting to the left of you. She is deliberately showing herself to me. That is unusual behavior for a person who hides behind masks. She is revealing some of her many masks—I am the flirt, the good mother, the good wife, the helpless woman, the business woman, the rich woman. I'm not book smart, but I am clever and my greatest strength is getting someone, usually a man, to get me what I want. I am good at hiding who I am, and I am very good at reading people. I won't come at you directly but from the left side. I have no compassion for my heart is a stone. I keep my eye on the gold ring. I am diabolical, greedy, destructive, and I don't give up. I want it all, and I want it now.

When he finished reading and looked up from text, I finished the story. "The psychic said she would like to put a protective barrier around me and asked if that was OK. She did a lot of magic talk and waved her hands around and said I was protected."

Brass kept quiet and I thought he was trying to keep from smiling. I know I would if I heard that from him. When he finally spoke, he sounded sincere. "What did you think about the psychic's apparition."

"It was creepy from the start and when she mentioned the Golden Eyelash Viper — she almost made me believe in God."

Brass's cell pinged. He had to get going and took me back to the hospital. Instead of goodbye he said, "Elle watch—your back."

CHAPTER 24 — CARLOTTA STONE

I haven't seen my kids in a couple of days. My life changed in a hurry as soon as I slapped that fat nurse. She asked for it. Now I'm under what feels like house arrest, Milo is in the hospital, and Piper is staying with her best friend.

This afternoon, Swainey drove me to UAMS so I could have a session with a psychiatrist. I'm not allowed to drive. JoAnne arranged this doctor visit after she explained her plans for me—the drug rehab clinic, therapy, the whole bullshit plan to keep me out of trouble after my performance at the hospital. I guess the doctor is also a teacher, because this is a medical school. I don't know, I didn't have my phone, so I can't look him up. Swainey checked me in and the receptionist took me back to meet Clinton Blankenship.

I was surprised at his office. It had a great view, and the sofa and chairs were high-end. I recognized them. I have the same ones in a different color. The area rug was one I'd seen at the same place where I got my sofa. I wanted it, but Mitch said no. He wouldn't pay a couple of grand for something that would end up being used as a giant pee pad for two dogs.

The decor made me feel good about Blankenship. We had something in common. He introduced himself and asked me to choose where I wanted to sit, and I picked the sofa. I was surprised he spoke with a slight accent. It sounded like he was from

England, but I didn't ask. Blankenship was tall, slim, and was probably blond before his hair went gray, and wore a beautiful dark blue cashmere sweater with relaxed-fit jeans. I could see him as a professor lecturing.

I'd only been to counseling one time and that was with Mitch, and I walked out after twenty minutes. He and the therapist were ganging up on me. She was a social worker/marriage counsellor, not a real doctor like Blankenship.

After I snuggled into the sofa, he said, "I have a variety of beverages to offer, if you would like—flat or sparkling water, soft drinks, fruit juices, tea, coffee. We'll be together about fifty minutes, and I want you to be comfortable."

"I'd like Diet Coke with a straw, if you have it," His receptionist brought the coke and a straw and an iced coffee for him. Then he got down to business.

He sat in a chair across from me and crossed his long legs. He took his time and had a few sips of his coffee before he said, "I spoke with JoAnne and she briefly explained the need for your visit. I'd like for you to tell me what is going on that caused the need for you to see me."

I was having a hard time reading him, which is unusual for me, so I didn't say anything. Blankenship waited, and I just looked at him. When I finally started to talk, I couldn't stop myself, I went on what Mitch would call a rapid-fire rant. “I feel like I’m under house arrest. I’m stuck in the house with my mother as my guard while JoAnne is going to put me in a rehab to keep me out of prison for slapping that nurse, so she says, but I wonder about that. I’m thinking I can’t trust her. I need to see Milo, but JoAnne said I have to wait until he is out of the hospital.”

I took a quick breath and started up again. “Piper didn’t go to school today because she said she was too embarrassed. She wants to move to another state, said that I had completely ruined her life here. She’s been shut up in her dance studio and won’t talk to me. And I’ve been thinking about JoAnne and mother’s plans for me, how they’re just like Mitch, so controlling. If I killed myself, which is probably what they want, whichever one took Milo and Piper would get a cool two hundred thousand a year to raise them. That’s incentive enough for me to stay alive, and to add them to my list of people who need their comeuppance.”

Blankenship looked down at his coffee and took another sip. I guess he was thinking about what to say. “I see you have a lot on your mind, and that’s understandable. We’ll take it a piece at a time.” So we started talking about what I said, and I found he made me feel like everything would be OK. He thought I was suffering from something like post-traumatic stress, and I would be fine, but needed help to get there.

That’s how I got started with Dr. Blankenship, and why I didn’t go to a fancy rehab clinic in California or jail. He recommended a place in Connecticut to JoAnne, and he said that she had already made arrangements and I would be admitted tomorrow. He told me how lucky I was to get in that quick. I felt like my daddy was speaking through him, and I did something I rarely do: I cried real tears—not ones I worked up when I needed them. I was looking forward to getting away for a while by myself. I needed a vacation from my life. I had to give JoAnne my power of attorney—I think that's what it's called—so she could take care of getting the house up to code and safe. She could do all that boring stuff for me.

After my session, Mother brought me back to The Playhouse. Piper wasn't there, and Mother said she was with Elle. I threw a fit, and Mother left the room and told me to grow up; she was "weary" of trying and failing to help me. She said, "This is out of yours hands now. Best if you just accept it."

"Best you accept it," sounded like a threat to me. Sort of like the "Go enjoy your empty future" text. I immediately called Peter Parsons and told him to start work on my appeal for the no-contest. He sounded off to me; like he was in a hurry to get off the phone, I wondered if he was going to quit. Can lawyers fire a client? After he said we had plenty of time to file an appeal, he said his office manager needed to speak with me and put me on hold. I hung up. He probably wanted me to pay the bills his office kept sending, and I didn't want to get into that discussion. I wasn't about to pay him for getting me kicked out of the trust. He needed to redeem himself by winning the appeal. I wasn't going to pay for something that wasn't finished, and this wasn't done.

I heard cars pull up, and then JoAnne talking to someone in the living room. I went downstairs, and my sister was speaking with a woman who wore tight fitting designer jeans and very expensive cashmere pullover. She introduced us. "Carlotta, this is Judy Evans, from social service. You know why she's here. I already explained that."

Evans extended her hand but I acted like I didn't notice. I could tell already I didn't like her. She looked a lot like Sylvia Parsons—big and athletic and with a smug look on her face. She thought she was better than me just because she was here. "And this is the house inspector." JoAnne indicated a man wearing a blue uniform.

"You can't come in here and boss my life around," I shook my index finger in my sister's face. I was pissed and she knew it. "If I need an inspector, I will hire one, not one you picked." I waved my hand at Evans, "As for you, really, a social worker." I didn't get to finish saying what was on my mind. Mother came into the room and said we needed to talk.

My mother and I went to the kitchen and, my sister and the case worker talked in the den, while the inspector looked around. He was gone quite a long time, looking in every room, under the house, in the basement, the garage. The kitchen was spotless, and so were the two bedrooms where Mother and JoAnne stayed when in town, but the rest of the house failed his inspection. "Infestation of rats and fleas in the basement area and under the crawl space, chewed wires, squirrels in the attic," and so on. He declared it wasn't safe.

JoAnne already had a solution; I should have known. I thought she would say the kids would live with her family in Fayetteville or they would go with my mother to Lonoke. What she did say put me through the roof.

"Judy Evans and I visited with the kids, and they want to stay with Elle at Izzy's house. I can't take them with me, and you can't expect Swainey to take them. They should stay in their school and move back to their own house when it's safe."

"Traitors—you've taken my kids and turned them against me." I wanted to throw my Coke can at them, but I knew better.

Mother tried to reason with me, "This is just temporary. No one is taking Milo and Piper. This is hard for me and for JoAnne too but . . . "

"Yack! Yack! Yack! Shut up! You must be brainwashed. I've never heard you say one good thing about Elle Hawk before, and now you're working with her or is it *for* her."

"Go enjoy your empty future," the curse rolled through my mind as I walked away from them and went upstairs.

CHAPTER 25 — ELLE HAWK

I woke up before dawn with a children's rhyme running through my mind.

Humpty Dumpty sat on a wall. Humpty Dumpty had a great fall. All the King's horses and all the King's men couldn't put Humpty back together again.

A big yellow moon shone in my face through the skylight over my head.

The day before, JoAnne and Carlotta left for the clinic in Connecticut. Birdie and I brought Milo and Piper out to Izzy's house. I was glad it was a weekend so the kids could settle in. On this morning, I went into the kitchen and heard a soft voice that sounded like my sister's. "Are you OK?" I jumped. "Are you OK?" It was Dizzy—her parrot. She'd named him after the horn player Dizzy Gillespie. "You OK?"

"I don't know. Are you OK?" I answered. Dizzy tilted his green head to the side like he was listening and opened his big yellow beak, and stretched his neck, and began to sing, "Oh, Shenandoah." I thought it appropriate, considering its history as an old work song.

What I had ahead of me, and the kids too, was work, hard work. I needed to find a way to build a new family for them, one that would hold once their mother returned.

Maybe all the king's horses and all the king's

men couldn't put Humpty back together again, but I wondered why bother to reconstruct something that couldn't sit on a wall without falling off whether it was a human, an egg like creature, or a cannon. I guess I'm skeptical. For the kids, I had hope—for their mother—not so much.

The kids needed a new kind of family, one that they helped design. They were old enough and smart enough to participate in building their future and it was my mission to see it happen.

I wanted to make sure my thinking was sound about my idea. I didn't want to start on a journey that went down the wrong road, so I consulted an old friend, a healer, who practiced family therapy in Eureka Springs, where he lived in a communal situation. I drove up to that quaint little town and spent the day with him. He helped me understand what was going on emotionally with the kids and how a sense of community would help them heal. I called Lee Edwards and left a short message about what I was needing. In about thirty minutes, I heard the familiar sounds of a helicopter circling and my cell rang.

"Thought I'd stop in, if you're okay with that. I can put her down in the pasture."

I went out on the deck and watched Edwards land the yellow helicopter on the field. He had a soft touch—so did Mitch. After the blades quit rotating and he got out, I waved to him. He jogged across the field toward the house. He's a graceful man.

Lee knew his way through the gardens, over the Koi pond's bridge, up the spiral steps, to the front door. I made him a double espresso and we sat down at the kitchen table and discussed my project. "I want you help me chose a staff from you list of *informants*. I envision a live-in older woman, who will manage the maid and the yard man, pay the household bills, and so on—a house manager. I will live in the house too so we can get the routine down with the kids before Carlotta is put back together again and returned to home."

Lee stood up and stretched his long, flexible body. Mitch used to do that after flying, Dizzy flew from the rafters and landed on his shoulder. Lee didn't flinch. "I saw him up in the skylight, and I've been waiting for him to come down and say hello to me."

On cue, the bird said, "Are you okay?" Lee presented his hand and Dizzy stepped on. "I know your type, you big flirt." Dizzy lowed his head and Lee rubbed the back of his neck. "Elle, you look shocked."

"I am. I thought most people were afraid of parrots."

"Grew up with various kinds of big birds. My mother's hobby was raising them and saving them. Now about what you need—it's a very tall order—but I think you might be in luck. The woman I have in mind just finished up five years working in a troubled family situation like you have here. I'll have to persuade her to move up from New Orleans. She won't be cheap. The maid and yard man will be easy."

Lee brought Alice Ford to Izzy's house to meet with me and Birdie a week later. We liked her right away. She reminded me of my grandmother, not in looks, but in the feel that came off her. Birdie said she reminded her of Mamaw Stone, her grandmother. I liked it that she had been a high school teacher before going into the nanny house keeper business. With WP's approval, Alice Ford joined our family.

After the house was made safe, the wires and gas leaks fixed and rats and raccoons gone, Alice moved to her quarters downstairs. I took the bedroom that was once Shelly's, and she took the bigger on the other side of the den between them. The house was cleared out of everything the kids didn't want, which was practically every piece of furniture except the big television. Alice took the kids to the paint store and they picked out the colors for their bedrooms. The living room stayed the same color. Milo said that was only fair to his mom, because she couldn't be here to decide. I liked that. Alice agreed it was a good sign.

The four of us went to Macy's and the kids chose the furniture for the den area of the kitchen, overstuffed furniture with lots of color that reminded me of what Mitch's girls had picked out before Carlotta came into their lives. Milo and Piper thought their mom should decide about the living room furniture, so we left it in place, but we did have the walls repainted the same color. Except for removing the hoarding and deep cleaning in the master suite, and refreshing the paint, we left Carlotta's closet, bathroom, and bedroom alone.

It was in the master bedroom that the handyman discovered in the wall behind the dresser a secret hiding place. It contained ten handguns and a bunch of dolls and lots of unidentified pills. I recognized the dolls that had once hung from the lynching tree. I removed everything and he sealed it off.

It took a while, but we went through all the boxes that were hidden under the couches, the beds, filling the closets, lining the hallways, and separating out the things we would send to various charities and what the kids wanted to keep. The stacked-up newspapers, magazines, and every other thing that should have been thrown in the trash years ago or recycled filled up three dumpsters. The Playhouse went through the same process,

Milo documented the whole process on his GoPro. He said he wasn't going to put it on YouTube, but he might need it later when his career as a screenwriter started up. I needed to connect him with Bill Brass. At first, I felt uncomfortable living in the house, and I didn't hide it. I told Piper and Milo, and they said they felt weird too. Being truthful with each other was a way of living that I was introducing to the kids. They were used to living with lies. I wanted them to learn to appreciate honesty in relationships.

After four months, Carlotta was ready to come home and I was worried. I asked WP to come by the house. We'd gotten to know each other better from working together, sorting out the logistics with the kids, JoAnne and Swainey, and we weren't finished yet as trustee and trust protector.

WP arrived the next morning after the kids had gone to school, Alice showed him in, and he whistled as he took in the new look of the house. I gave him a tour; he hadn't been there since it was finished. He said the house looked like a happy place to raise kids. We sat down at the kitchen table and Alice brought coffee and biscotti. WP picked up a manila envelope sitting there with his name on it. "Before you open this," I nodded to the envelope, "I want to talk about Carlotta." He put it back down on the table.

"I got a disturbing call from JoAnne. She is going to Connecticut to bring her sister home in a few days. Carlotta wants to take a private jet and JoAnne asked if I thought the kids' trust would pay for it. That put me on alert. I told her to call you; it wasn't up to me. Do you think JoAnne is back enabling her?"

"I thought you and JoAnne worked pretty well together, considering the history you have with her, and you know her better than I do."

"The only thing I'm sure of is the dynamic is going to change when Carlotta comes home. JoAnne doesn't want to take over raising the kids, and Swainey isn't up to it. I saw her at Kroger, and she rides in one of those shopping carts with the basket on it. She needs a knee replacement. Carlotta is wanting to be the local Kardashian as usual and arrive in a private jet and that makes me think she plans to go back to her old ways."

"I'll approve the children's trust paying for JoAnne as a companion to accompany their mother home, but not a private jet. They'll have to travel commercial or pay the difference from their own pocketbooks. How's it going with the housekeeper? Is all that still good? It better be. She's certainly not cheap. Only reason I approved that big expense is Mitch would have seen it as essential."

"The kids are crazy about Alice, especially her home cooking, plus she helps Piper with her homework and teaches her even more than what she learns at school—she's like a private tutor. Another thing that makes me feel better about Carlotta coming back is Judy Evans' and social services are still involved."

WP waited a while before saying anything at all. He didn't seem to be in a hurry for a busy attorney. "I'm hoping the time she spent in rehab and that fancy psychiatric clinic has rehabilitated her. That's bound to change her for the good. Don't you think?"

"You know who has really changed—Milo. You getting him involved with a Scout troop was a good move. Mitch would approve. He's made some good friends and your younger son has become a mentor to him. But you know that. Milo loves riding dirt bikes out at the quarry with him. And Piper's behavior at school has changed and they are letting her stay. Alice is the one responsible for that turn around."

WP asked, "The changes in the kids—is that due to the therapy sessions or to you and their new living arrangement?"

"I think both plus the kids are back doing things with the cousins. But I'm worried what will happen when Carlotta comes back."

"It's hard to know—have to wait and see. What are your plans once Carlotta gets settled back into her life? Are you going back to Hawaii?" He got up and put his mug in the sink and rinsed it. WP looked like he was getting ready to leave.

"I'll be living with Izzy for a while. She's asked me to move in. I won't leave Little Rock until I'm positive the kids are OK. I want to take Piper and Milo to Maui for a month this summer. Once I leave here, my home base will be Cinci, but who knows for how long."

Kelpe picked up the envelope. "Last time I got one of these from you, it took me a year before I remembered to open it, and then it changed my life. Don't know if I want to open this one." But he did.

WP pulled out the book. On the cover was an Audubon-type drawing of a red-tailed hawk holding a small yellow snake in its talons. Kelpe opened *THE TRUST PROTECTOR* by Elle Hawk and said, "Am I looking at the next shit show?"

Alice suddenly appeared in front of us, "We've got a big problem outside." WP and I stood up and headed toward the front door.

"No! The back yard, out by the pool," Alice pointed toward the windows in the den area of the kitchen.

Kelpe and I walked toward the wall of windows. Dressed in all black, from her hoodie to her stretch pants to her high heel boots, Carlotta sat in a lawn chair. A Diet Coke with a straw was on the table next to her. She had a small red box in her lap and was looking down at her phone. I touched WP's arm. "I thought she was still in Connecticut?"

"So did I." He scrolled through his contacts and made a call. "JoAnne, your sister is sitting by the pool. What's up? I thought you were going to go get her in a couple of days."

While WP was on the phone, I stepped away and called Bill Brass. I didn't want WP to hear me or know I even knew the detective. I hung up and walked out to the laundry room and told Alice to call 9-1-1 and report an intruder. She hesitated, looked at me with a question in her eyes, and made the call.

WP finished and filled me in. "JoAnne said Carlotta called the other day and said she was coming home on her own."

"Why didn't she tell us?"

"She thought Carlotta sounded fine and she didn't want to over-manage her. She was going to call but hadn't gotten around to it."

"She keeps pointing that red box at the house. What's that supposed to mean? It feels like a threat, like she's pointing a gun at us."

Alice spoke up, "I'll go see what's up? It would be natural for me to since I'm the housekeeper and there is a stranger in the yard. I haven't met her yet. I could introduce myself."

"No! Wait for the police."

"What! Why did you call the cops? We don't need more drama." WP was losing some of his signature cool.

"Something is going on. I feel it. We need witnesses in case she's up to something. Think! What normal person would be acting like this."

"Don't you think you are being a little paranoid."

"WP! She hired some kind of personal retribution service to hurt me and I got lucky. Wake up and get you head out of your ass. Look what she did to your personal life. She's a fuckin' nut. She knows we're in the house—our cars are parked out front. This is one of her games. I'm guessing, any minute now one of us is going to get a text or call from an unknown number." I was interrupted when my phone vibrated—a text from Brass. "I'm here—stay put."

WP's cell pinged. He read the text out loud. "WP did you really think I would let you and the *trust protector* steal my life." He looked at me and Alice, "I thought she was rehabilitated. Look, she's waving that red box at the house again. What's that supposed to mean?"

"I don't know. She looks crazy. Are you going to respond?"

"No, that's exactly what she wants. Better to ignore her. She's a whole lot like our President—everything is all about her. I'm not going to feed the beast. If she wants to engage me, she'll have to walk into the house."

The pool guy arrived, it wasn't the usual man,

and I wondered if it was one of Brass' guys. He started cleaning the filters. I kept the pool heated this time of year and swam laps to keep me sane.

Carlotta walked up to him. It looked like she was telling him to leave. He motioned to his ears and started signing her. She pointed toward the steps. From her body language, it looked like she was yelling at him and he kept signing. She gave up and went back to her chair

A tall man in blue jeans, wearing cowboy boots, a hiking vest over a khaki shirt walked down the steps to the pool. It was Brass. My cell vibrated. I heard Brass say, "I'll keep the line open." I saw him put the phone in his vest pocket.

Carlotta's back was to him and he waited for her to turn around. Brass introduced himself and she said, "Are you that cop who came here about the gas leak?"

"Good memory," He didn't say anything more.

"Is there another problem here at the house? If there is, it's not my fault. I've been on vacation for months. I just got home."

"There might be. Call came in to 9-1-1, the house keeper told the operator there was an intruder, and she was frightened."

"I haven't met her yet. I just got back and haven't been inside the house. I better go and introduce myself. You can run along now."

Brass picked the red box up from the table. Carlotta reached for it but she wasn't quick enough to pluck it from his hand, "That's mine! Put it down." Brass opened the box, took a long look, and handed it to her.

"I don't know what's in there. It doesn't belong to me."

Brass said, "I just heard you say this box was yours."

"I did not say that! That box was sitting on this table when I got here. It's mine because it is on my property. It probably belongs to my mother-in-law, Elle Hawk. She's been watching my kids while I've been on vacation. You need to get off my property."

Two athletic looking men dressed in black tee shirts and black jeans walked down the steps toward them and handed Brass something in a metal box. Carlotta brushed past them. Brass took her by the arm. She drew back her hand like she was going to slap him but stopped when she saw a uniformed officer behind the men.

The phone went dead. Brass must have turned it off. There was what looked like, based on the body language, a heated discussion, and then the officer cuffed Carlotta, with her hands behind her back, and took her away. Brass walked off with the men and soon we heard a knock at the front door. Alice went to see about it. I heard Brass introduce himself and asked if I was home.

"Elle, I'm going back to the office—right now. I don't want anything to do with this, whatever this is." WP walked toward the front door. He left my gift on the table but turned came back and picked it up. He waved the envelope at me smiled and said, "Not going to make the same mistake twice."

WP met up with Brass in the entry hall. I stayed in the kitchen. I didn't want him to know my connection with Brass. There was a short discussion between them and WP left.

Brass walked into the kitchen. I was so glad to see him that I wanted to hug him and I don't usually touch people, but I contained myself. He took a seat at the table. Alice brought us tall iced orange juice, lemon cookies, and left to go to the grocery store.

I waited for Brass to start his report. I could see he was lining it up his mind— how much he wanted to tell me. I told myself to listen and not interrupt with the dozens of questions running through my mind.

"I got a call from Lee the other day. You know that he still monitors the cameras around the place and has added a few more discreet ones outside. Three men entered the property and disabled the obvious cameras. The remaining ones recorded men entering the house while you and Alice were gone and the kids were at school. After the intruders left, Lee's men came out, looked around, found explosives, and called me. We disabled what was found. The red box held a detonator. This morning, the camera showed Carlotta entering the property, taking the box from the garage, and going down to the pool area. You know the rest."

"Was she going to blow up the house?"

"Well, she couldn't if she wanted to since we took care of it. She was probably told not to be near the place when she did set it off. But it doesn't appear the goal was to blast the house off the face of the earth. The charges were designed to create damage that a house would get from a strong earthquake. It was meant to frighten and hurt who ever was inside when it went off."

"Why do you think she came here and let us see her?"

"She couldn't resist taunting you, that's my guess. The cameras show her removing the box and that's proof she knew it was there. I hate to think what might have happened if Lee hadn't of been on the job."

"Remember the lynching tree? Parsons and Kelpe were hanging from it. Someone needs to check on their homes." I shook my head and made a little laugh. “All those cameras will take her down. She’s put a noose around her own neck again. What do you think is going to happen to her?”

“She’s down at the station, and her sister’s on her way. Someone from the department will handle it from here—not me.”

“I don’t mean today. What’s going to happen to her further down the road. She is practically a home grown terrorist. We don’t know what she has in store for Parsons or Kelpe. Blowing up her own house—sick.”

“Elle, I can’t read her future. But I do know that the Golden Eyelash Viper will not be able to out run *The Long Arm of The Law*.”